Cambridge

Elements in Austr~~~ ~~~~~~~~
edited by
Peter Boettke
George Mason University

CULTURAL CONSIDERATIONS WITHIN AUSTRIAN ECONOMICS

Virgil Storr
George Mason University, Virginia

Arielle John
George Mason University, Virginia

CAMBRIDGE
UNIVERSITY PRESS

CAMBRIDGE
UNIVERSITY PRESS

University Printing House, Cambridge CB2 8BS, United Kingdom

One Liberty Plaza, 20th Floor, New York, NY 10006, USA

477 Williamstown Road, Port Melbourne, VIC 3207, Australia

314–321, 3rd Floor, Plot 3, Splendor Forum, Jasola District Centre,
New Delhi – 110025, India

79 Anson Road, #06–04/06, Singapore 079906

Cambridge University Press is part of the University of Cambridge.

It furthers the University's mission by disseminating knowledge in the pursuit of
education, learning, and research at the highest international levels of excellence.

www.cambridge.org
Information on this title: www.cambridge.org/9781108708166
DOI: 10.1017/9781108761505

© Virgil Storr and Arielle John 2020

First published 2020

A catalogue record for this publication is available from the British Library.

ISBN 978-1-108-70816-6 Paperback
ISSN 2399-651X (online)
ISSN 2514-3867 (print)

Cultural Considerations within Austrian Economics

Elements in Austrian Economics

DOI: 10.1017/9781108761505
First published online: June 2020

Virgil Storr
George Mason University, Virginia

Arielle John
George Mason University, Virginia

Author for correspondence: Virgil Storr, vstorr@gmu.edu

Abstract: Increasingly, economists are realizing that a deeper understanding of culture can improve their insights into the most important questions in economics. The Austrian school of political economy, which has always taken economics to be a science of meaning, and therefore, a science of culture, offers a unique approach to the study of culture in economic life. The authors consider three important differences between these Austrian and non-Austrian approaches: the Austrian focus on culture as meaning rather than culture as norms, beliefs, or attitudes; the Austrian emphasis on culture as an interpretative lens rather than as a tool or form of capital; and the Austrian insistence that cultural analysis be a qualitative exercise rather than a quantitative one. They also examine Geertz's description of culture, Gadamer's approach to hermeneutics, and Weber's interpretative sociology, demonstrating their connections to the Austrian approach and offering examples of what Austrian cultural economics can look like.

Keywords: culture and economics; institutions; entrepreneurship; Max Weber; interpretive

ISBNs: 9781108708166 (PB), 9781108761505 (OC)
ISSNs: 2399-651X (online), 2514-3867 (print)

Contents

1 Introduction

The relationship between culture and economic action is an intimate one. Culture is a pattern of shared meaning, a context in which all of life is rendered intelligible, a lens through which we view and make sense of the world. Culture can affect whether or not entrepreneurs identify certain opportunities, how they evaluate those opportunities and the strategies for exploiting those opportunities that entrepreneurs adopt. Culture also likely shapes the way that economic actors understand the formal institutions that constrain their actions and incentivizes or disincentivizes certain behaviors. As such, a greater understanding of the role of culture has the potential to improve our understanding of the most important questions in economics.

Since culture can shape economic action and outcomes, economists should, arguably, reference culture in their analysis. Still, many economists are reticent to do so. Some feel that culture is too murky a concept to be operationalized by economists. Mokyr (2017: 8), for example, while not hesitant to study culture, notes that, for many economists, "[c]ulture is a vague and mushy word," with a "mind-boggling number of definitions employed." Others argue that preference-based explanations belong squarely in the domain of anthropology and other social scientists, hence economists are meant to be using 'economic' explanations to study economic phenomena and not appealing to culture. Some economists also choose to focus on institutions and incentives in order to explain differences in behavior, and hence see culture as a different type of force not worthy of economic investigation.

There are, of course, exceptions; several of them quite notable.[1] Guiso et al. (2006), for instance, pointed to differences in cultures to explain differences in economic progress across countries. They conclude that culture shapes the beliefs and values people hold regarding their economic decisions, and that those decisions in turn affect economic progress. In particular, the authors argue that people who value thrift save more, and that richer societies are the ones where people save more. They find, for instance, that "an increase of one standard deviation in the share of people who think educating children to thriftiness increases the saving rate by 1.8 percentage point increase in the national saving rate" (2006: 39). Additionally, Guiso et al. (2009) argue that culture influences a group's trust in and willingness to trade with foreigners. The authors relied on the results of surveys from Europe that were constructed to gauge and compare how much citizens trusted their fellow citizens and how

---

[1] See also Knack and Keefer (1997), La Porta et al. (1997), Throsby (1999, 2001), Bertrand et al. (2000), Henrich et al. (2001), Bertrand and Schoar (2006), Fisman and Miguel (2007), Algan and Cahuc (2009, 2010), Fehr and Leibbrandt (2011), Gorodnichenko and Roland (2011, 2017), and Alesina and Guiliano (2015).

much they trusted foreigners. The authors further argue that where two societies have high bilateral levels of trust, those countries will have high levels of trade, foreign direct investment, and portfolio investment between each other. As such, since culture influences trust, culture therefore explains economic interdependence, integration, and success.

Similarly, Tabellini (2008, 2010) examined the relationship between culture and morality, and morality and transactions. He compared cultures with "generalized morality," that is, cultures where people are willing to treat all others in their society according to norms of good conduct and willing to respect their political rights, to cultures with "limited morality," where opportunistic and selfish behavior toward "outsiders" is rampant, and rights and benefits are extended to just a privileged few, like one's family members. To get at generalized morality, Tabellini examines and compares how strongly societies value trust, respect for others, teaching obedience in the family, and personal control over one's life. He finds that societies that value trust, respect, obedience, and personal control highly tend to exhibit higher economic growth and development.

Austrian economists have not been reluctant to highlight the role of culture in shaping economic actions and outcomes. In fact, a concern for culture (albeit sometimes not invoking the term) has long been a consideration among Austrian economists. Menger (1892: 255), for instance, famously pointed out that money, far from something with objective significance and value, "has not been generated by law. In its origin it is a social, and not a state institution." Which objects come to be viewed and treated as money in a given context depends on culture, among other things. Similarly, Mises stressed the importance of focusing on thymology, which he described as "what a man knows about the way in which people value different conditions, about their wishes and desires and their plans to realize these wishes and desires" (1957: 271–272). Thymology could answer why someone would prefer water to wine, for example, as this was decidedly not an economic matter for Mises.

Hayek, for his part, focused the role of cultural evolution and argued that facts of social science were not statistics or objects per se, but the thoughts and beliefs in people's mind about the world. For Hayek (1973: 17), much of our ability to navigate the world depends on us having culture,

> The cultural heritage into which man is born consists of a complex of practices or rules of conduct which have prevailed because they made a group of men successful but which were not adopted because it was known that they would bring about desired effects. Man acted before he thought and did not understand before he acted. What we call understanding

is in the last resort simply his capacity to respond to his environment with a pattern of actions that helps him to persist.

Hayek (1973: 22) also believed that cultural anthropology was the intellectual tradition in which the academic understanding of social evolution "has been most fruitfully developed."

More recently, Lavoie (2011: 107), a strong proponent of cultural explanation in economics, has argued that "when we study human societies the purposes we attribute to the objects of our examination are not metaphorical but real and already meaningful to them. We are able to view them 'from the inside.'" Stated alternately, studying human societies means studying culture. Lavoie (1991: 36), for instance, has suggested that understanding entrepreneurship means recognizing that "entrepreneurship ... is primarily a cultural process. The seeing of profit opportunities is a matter of cultural interpretation." Similarly, Lavoie and Chamlee-Wright (2000: 69) have argued that,

> the spirit of enterprise comes in many different flavors. Each culture creates a unique entrepreneurial pattern; each culture articulates its own genre of stories in which economic leaders achieve wealth-generating success within the specific institutional and customary contours of the society in which they live.

Several other Austrians, including Boettke (1998a) and Storr (2004, 2013), have also focused on culture to understand economic phenomena. Given the primacy of institutions for economic development, Boettke (1998a) argues that to understand which institutions will "stick" in a particular society, we first need to understand the culture of the people living there, where culture is defined as "those beliefs and practices which give institutions legitimacy" (Boettke 1998a: 12). As Boettke (1998: 14) states, in pursuing our analysis, "we have to find a way to understand the ideas, beliefs, habits that are indigenous to an area, and then see how the political, legal, and economic institutions that are correlated with economic development fit in the social ecology." Only by studying a society's history and culture, Boettke contends, can economists gain insight into the society's functioning; imposing culturally incompatible rules on those societies will not lead to economic success. Furthermore, Storr (2013) sees culture as thoroughly coloring economic life, and advocates for economists to "make every effort to understand how individuals actually experience markets" (2013: 99). Understanding the spirits that animate markets, Storr explains, involves understanding the meanings that people attribute to the world and the lessons that they learn as they go through life.

The Austrian school of political economy takes economics to be a science of meaning and so a science of culture. In fact, the Austrian methodological approach, known as praxeology, takes culture seriously and examines it from a unique standpoint. This project explores the uniqueness of the Austrian approach to the study of culture in economic life. We will argue that the Austrian approach to studying culture differs in important respects from non-Austrian efforts. We focus on three differences between Austrian and non-Austrian approaches: the Austrian focus on culture as meaning rather than culture as norms and attitudes, the Austrian emphasis on culture as an interpretive lens rather than as a tool, and the Austrian insistence that cultural analysis be a qualitative exercise rather than as a quantitative effort. In Section 2, we examine the relationship between Gadamer's approach to hermeneutics, Weberian interpretative sociology, and their connections to the Austrian approach to including cultural considerations into economic analysis, offering examples of what cultural analysis in that vein can look like. Next, Section 3 reviews several studies by non-Austrian economists that explore the relationship between culture and economic action. Section 4 then considers important differences between Austrian and non-Austrian approaches to studying culture and economic action. In Section 5, we review several studies by Austrian economists that explore the relationship between culture and economic action. Finally, Section 6 offers concluding remarks.

2 The Intellectual Roots of the Austrian Approach to Culture

2.1 An Approach Rooted in Hermeneutics

Providing a thoughtful challenge to orthodox economic methodology, Don Lavoie published an essay called "The Interpretive Dimension of Economics: Science, Hermeneutics, and Praxeology" in 1985 (Lavoie 2011). Lavoie wished to achieve two goals with that essay. First, he wanted to emphasize that all scientific endeavors required acts of interpretation, as he believed scientists tended to underestimate or ignore that essential requirement. Second, Lavoie wanted to demonstrate that Austrian economics was the branch of economics that took the interpretive requirement the most seriously. By the "interpretive" requirement, Lavoie meant that part of doing social science was to observe how people interpreted their worlds – to observe the meanings that they read into events and the meanings that they attributed to their own actions and those of others. Lavoie understood that human beings acted with intention. Thus, social scientists did not need to impose intentions onto people or presume motivations for them. Rather, the job of the social scientist was to learn their subjects' intentions, or rather to interpret their subjects' "*already* interpreted meanings" (2011: 106). This systematic investigation of people's interpretations, this science of explaining meanings, was called *hermeneutics*. As Lavoie stated, when we study human societies the purposes we attribute to the objects of our examination are not metaphorical but real and already meaningful to them. We are able to view them "from the inside." Richard Zaner (1974, p. 392) noted that "the social world is experienced as already constituted and meaningful by each of us in our daily lives." Or as Gadamer (1976, p. 15) said, "There is always a world already interpreted, already organized in its basic relations, into which experience steps." The task of the social scientist is to find and explicate a meaning that is always already there, rather than to invent a merely metaphorical "meaning" which works in predictive tests. (2011: 107)

Lavoie emphasized that scientists possessed no special ability to read others' minds and to access their intentions. Indeed, Lavoie (2011: 109) argued that hermeneutics as a method was "not fundamentally different from the method by which we understand our fellow man in everyday life, but is simply intended to represent a more careful and systematic effort." A necessary step for such careful interpretation, he argued was communication or dialogue with subjects or the cultural texts that they authored or embraced. Lavoie, therefore, privileged qualitative methods in social science.

Of course, one concern with this method was that scientists could too easily bring their prejudiced perspectives into conversations with their subjects, sullying the data with overly rosy or cynical interpretations of people's words. Mathematical and statistical tools were seen as providing proper defenses against sloppy subjectivism. Lavoie strongly disagreed with that position. He pointed out that people's prejudices could only be confronted, never sidestepped with the use of statistical techniques. He insisted that both the subject's and the researcher's interpretations were important inputs into the generation of scientific knowledge. As Lavoie (2011: 109) stated, "we can neither ignore our object's point of view, nor escape our own and adopt his." Moreover, the only avenue available for a researcher to improve upon their misinterpretations was a process of rigorous and honest dialogue with their subjects, as well as other members of the scientific community.

Finally, Lavoie explained why statistics did not necessarily remove subjectivity and interpretation from science. For one, statistics simply do not capture a subject's interpretations, which for Lavoie were the primary object to be explored in social science. In addition, statistics do not offer insights into why one scientific explanation might be superior to another. Statistics are only constructed after interpretation takes place, that is, after a scientist has made a judgment call about what things need measuring and how. Quoting Gadamer, Lavoie says (2011: 112),

> Gadamer's remarks about statistics underscore the need for the interpretive
> dimension of even the most quantitative research. 'Statistics provides us with
> a useful example of how the hermeneutical dimension encompasses the entire
> procedure of science ... [W]hat is established by statistics seems to be
> a language of facts, but which questions these facts answer and which facts
> would begin to speak if other questions were asked are hermeneutical ques-
> tions (1976, p. 11)'.

In short, for Lavoie, scientists had no choice but to embrace subjectivity in their
data, dialogue in their methods, and "storytelling" as a means of persuading
their peers (2011: 113).

Lavoie argued that Austrian economics was the most promising strain of
neoclassical economics for applying hermeneutics. This was because
Austrian economics was mostly free of the "objectivist bias" found in neoclassical economics, a bias that held that the interpretive parts of scientific
explanation were subsidiary or inferior to the predictive part. In the extreme
objectivist position, what made science "science" was prediction, not interpretation. Scientific explanations had to be grounded in data or "facts" that
were objective and unequivocal in order to protect scientific explanations
from degenerating into relativism (the acceptance that "anything goes") and
"to rid reasoning of all ambiguities, to rid researchers of all biases, to rid
scientific disciplines of alternative schools or perspectives" (2011: 99).
Neoclassical economists, Lavoie argued, believed that mathematics and statistics empowered them to provide precise predictions and therefore to be
scientific. For those economists, to not present a theory using formal math,
and to not "test" that theory using econometrics, was to not do science.
Lavoie advanced several arguments to demonstrate the error in thinking that
facts were sterile phenomena, detached of subjectivity and devoid of human
interpretation (2011: 101). For Lavoie,

> The only 'test' any theory can receive is in the form of a qualitative judgment
> of the plausibility of the sequence of events that has been strung together by
> narrative. Theoretical sciences like economics can supply the principles of
> explanation but only the historical narrative can put these principles to work
> and establish their applicability and significance in some specific concrete
> circumstances under investigation. (2011: 113)

The virtue of Austrian economics for Lavoie was that it avoided the objectivist
bias and focused on the interpretive features of economic explanation, namely
"the historical (both history proper and history of ideas), linguistic, narrative,
dialogical, perspectivistic, tacit, and sociological aspects of economic explanation" (1991: 92). For one, Austrians held subjective value to be paramount.
They insisted that "value and other economic phenomena are to be explained by

reference to the subjective meaning attached to them by individual human minds" (2011: 116).

Lavoie argued that an endorsement of hermeneutics was consistent with praxeology and could be found within the various epistemological positions of Austrian economist Ludwig von Mises (2011: 117–124). For example, Mises held that the economic significance of various events and objects did not lie in their physical properties (like the round shape and the metallic composition of money, or the numerical representation of a price or quantity of a product) but in people's subjective assessments of those events and objects, which were the true data to be captured. Mises also believed that various facts of history could not be plucked from "objective" data sets in order to substantiate various theories, but that theories could only be refined through a process of interpretation and scientific dialogue. Lavoie proposed that Austrians more than other economists respected the interpretive aspects of economic explanation, a theme that one could also observe in Hayek's writings about the role of tradition in the economy. Lavoie further pointed out that Austrian economists tended to do applied work using case studies and narrative history, and that they preferred using words to describe both their theories and their empirics, as opposed to equations and statistics (2011: 116). For all of these reasons, Lavoie concluded that "[t]he methodology Austrian economists call praxeology can be seen in turn as exemplary of a hermeneutical approach to economics" (2011: 92).

As Storr (2011) describes, Lavoie's essay, comprising "the most extensive statement of Lavoie's position" on hermeneutics, subsequently triggered a debate on hermeneutics among Austrian economics. According to Storr, while some Austrians welcomed Lavoie's call for Austrian economics to accept and embrace its interpretive foundations, others rejected the existence of those foundations. On balance, however, Storr suggests, the reaction to Lavoie's paper was "overwhelmingly negative" (2011: 86). Prominent Austrian economists, including Murray Rothbard, accused the hermeneutical approach of historicism, relativism, and nihilism. They claimed that Lavoie's position was at best irrelevant and at worst heretical to economics. "For Rothbard," Storr (2011: 86) pointed out, "embracing hermeneutics means rejecting economics."

Despite this opposition, Lavoie's later work clarified why embracing the interpretive dimension of economics, in general, and a focus on culture and cultural processes, in particular, would permit a richer understanding of the entrepreneurial market process, a cornerstone of Austrian economic theory. According to Lavoie (1991), a full appreciation of the role of the entrepreneur and cultural considerations were naturally missing from the neoclassical theory of markets due to several unrealistic foundations of neoclassical economics. For one, Lavoie argued, neoclassical theory began by focusing on a hypothetical

Robinson Crusoe – an isolated individual attempting to apply means to achieve given ends. Although Friday was eventually brought into the analysis, Lavoie argued that the primary focus on an individual absent from society, an individual whose means and ends are determined prior to any social process, was misguided. Secondly, neoclassical economists ascribed to a "static" and "fully mechanistic" vision of the economy (1991: 41). In this vision, culture is simply that which determines what goods people want (hence it is out of the scope of economic theory), while entrepreneurship is mostly an exercise in computing "quantitative facts" relating to profits. Thus, in the neoclassical model, the market works like a "clockwork mechanism" (1991: 35), with no room for culture, and only a barebones theory of entrepreneurship.

Austrian economists filled a critical gap in economic theory by introducing the theory of the entrepreneurial market process. Lavoie notes that Kirzner was correct to elevate the importance of entrepreneurial *discovery* in markets, to demonstrate that important information about the economy (prices offered, quantities demanded, etc.) were not simply objective givens that a robot could calculate but required alertness to the particular economic circumstances in order to be perceived (1991: 40). However, for Lavoie, market process theory was incomplete without an examination of culture and cultural change. Lavoie noted that while Mises and Kirzner did not, like the mainstream neoclassical economists, ignore the role of entrepreneurship, they were not fully embracing of an interpretive economics (1991: 43). Kirzner's entrepreneur was primarily meant to equilibrate demand and supply. Lavoie rejected this notion of entrepreneurship as an equilibrating mechanism for the economy. He instead tried to show that markets should be more fully considered as an example of "open-ended genuinely creative and evolutionary processes, rather than mechanisms that focus on a predetermined end state" (1991: 43).

For Lavoie, markets are deeply cultural phenomena. Any examination of markets and of entrepreneurship would, thus, be incomplete without an exploration of the culture involved. "Entrepreneurship necessarily takes place within culture," he insisted, "it is utterly shaped by culture, and it fundamentally consists in interpreting and influencing culture" (1991: 35). Lavoie further maintained that "[m]arkets can be viewed as offshoots of, and complements to, the process of cultural dynamics" (1991: 51).

Relying on Gadamer's philosophy of hermeneutics and his concept of the close relationship between mind, thought, and language, Lavoie argued that culture should

> be understood broadly as the complex of meanings that allows us to comprehend human action: is it the background context that renders purposeful

action intelligible. Culture is the language in which past events are interpreted, future circumstances are anticipated, and plans of action are formu-
lated. Although not a language in the sense of a static sense of a static set of
words and grammatical rules, culture is a discourse. (1991: 34)

From this view of culture as a background context that provides a way of
interpreting the world, Lavoie explains why the Robinson Crusoe framework
associated with neoclassical economics was an erroneous foundation for social
theory. People are always first and foremost part of society, Lavoie argued,
steeped in a culture, interacting with other minds, and learning how to interpret
the world from these interactions. Citing Gadamer, Lavoie points out that "the
mind is already social before it is rational" (1991: 48), hence market activity
never emerges out of the blue, from the mind of a single person, but through
mutual interaction within the context of a culture. Just as Crusoe is not "cul-
tureless," successful entrepreneurs are not loners (as perhaps the popular conceptions imagine) but are people who are "especially well plugged into the
culture" (1991: 49).

Thus, while Lavoie believed Kirzner's focus on the *discovery* of entrepreneurial opportunities was useful, Kirzner's theory was incomplete for Lavoie
because it did not give sufficient weight to the process of *interpretation* of
entrepreneurial opportunities. For Lavoie, people do not mechanically recognize things in the world as profit opportunities in some objective sense. Rather,
people subjectively assess what they experience in a multitude of ways. Two
people with two different interpretive frameworks may perceive and interpret
the world before them differently. As Lavoie stated, "the profit opportunities the
entrepreneur discovers are not directly copied off of reality in itself; they are
interpreted from a point of view" (1991: 44). Tracing this insight back to
Gadamer's concept on language, Lavoie notes that market interaction is much
like linguistic interaction, and hence that interpretation and communication are
the linchpins of market activity. As he notes,

> Different entrepreneurial acts are the readings of, and contributions to,
> different conversations. The successful supplier of consumer goods listens
> to the discourse of the consuming public, senses what they will be likely to
> find attractive and what they will not, and is thereby more persuasive in
> getting them to try new products. The successful venture capitalist listens to
> the concerns of the banking community and thereby enhances his ability to
> persuade the loan officer to make an investment. The successful supplier of
> innovative industrial inputs listens to the technology conversations of his
> potential customers, exploits his skill in anticipating their specific require-
> ments, and thereby gains an ability to persuade them to explore hitherto
> ignored technological possibilities. The successful employer listens to the
> discourse of existing and potential employees and tries to shape an attractive

work environment that will persuade new workers to come and old ones to stay. What make entrepreneurs successful is their ability to join conversational processes and nudge them in new directions. (1991: 50)

Furthermore, a focus on cultural processes and cultural evolution can inform our understanding of economic change. For Lavoie, the interpretation of profit opportunities is an active process: "Profit opportunities are not so much like road signs to which we assign an automatic meaning as they are like difficult texts in need of a sustained effort of interpretation. Entrepreneurship is not only a matter of opening one's eyes, of switching on one's attentiveness; it requires directing one's gaze" (1991: 46). People's interpretive frameworks, their cultures, matter for what they see, what they don't see, and how they assess what's in front of them. As people's interpretative frameworks change (e.g., as their social stock of knowledge grows with new life experiences and new interactions), or as they attempt to change them, they begin to discover and act on different opportunities. In turn, their markets begin look different.

Recalling Lavoie, facts do not speak for themselves, rather, they are interpreted through a cultural lens. By gaining a better understanding of the cultural lens through which research subjects interpret their circumstances, the researcher gains a better understanding of why the actions they observe makes sense to the actors. This in turn allows the researcher to render complex phenomena more intelligible, which, to an Austrian, is the point of economic analysis. Lavoie's insights on culture and entrepreneurship contributed to the development of much of the applied cultural work in Austrian economics referenced in Section 4.

2.2 An Approach Rooted in Weber

The approach to studying the relationship between culture and economic action adopted by Austrian economists is rooted in the approach advanced by Max Weber. Max Weber's connections to Austrian economists like Carl Menger, Eugene Bohm-Bahwerk, and Ludwig von Mises are quite deep (Boettke 1998b, Boettke and Storr 2002, Zafirovski 2002, Storr 2004). In addition to his sociological studies, Weber was interested in questions of economic theory and methodology, and his understanding and defense of marginal utility theory clearly derived from the Austrian school (Weber 1975 [1908]).[2] Further, like the Austrians, Weber was also committed to

---

[2] Later, another Austrian economist, Ludwig von Mises would point out that Weber, thanks to his "ingenious intuition," correctly understood the theory of marginal utility (1949: 126). Mises added that "[i]f Weber had known the term "praxeology," he probably would have preferred it" (1949: 126).

methodological subjectivism (Boettke 1998b: 68). For instance, Weber explained that people fuse or impose meaning on the world, as opposed to objects or events having intrinsic meaning in and of themselves. Similarly, the Austrian school maintained that goods have no inherent value, and that a good only has "utility" for a person if the person believes that using the thing would remove some of their uneasiness.

Weber's understanding of economics mirrored the Austrian approach. For Weber, economics demonstrated that people act to try to alleviate tensions or dissatisfactions (1975 [1908]: 27). Economics was concerned with the problems that people grappled with as they attempted to satisfy their wants and needs, namely, that goods were scarce, and that people had to compete with each other for them. As Weber explained,

> Marginal utility theory … treats human action as if it ran its course from beginning to end under the control of commercial calculation – a calculation set up on the basis of all conditions that need to be considered. It treats individual 'needs' and the goods available (or to be produced or to be exchanged) for their satisfaction as mathematically calculable 'sums' and 'amounts' in a continuous process of bookkeeping. It treats man as an agent who constantly carries on 'economic enterprise', and it treats his life as the object of his 'enterprise' controlled according to calculation. The outlook involved in commercial bookkeeping is, if anything, the starting point of the constructions of marginal utility theory. For its purposes, marginal utility theory treats the 'psyche' of all men (conceived of as isolated entities and regardless of whether they are involved in buying and selling) as a merchant's soul, which can assess quantitatively the 'intensity' of its needs as well as the available means of their satisfaction. It is in this way that the theory attains to its theoretical constructions. (1975 [1908]: 31–32)

Like the Austrian economists, Weber held an *analytical* notion of the individual as a commercial calculator engaged in economic enterprise, having "a merchant's soul." He noted that this notion of the individual was only an "ideal type" – an abstraction from reality and a conceptual construction useful for analyzing real people situated in various cultural-historical circumstances. Like the Austrians, too, Weber thought it was indeed necessary to focus on these circumstances. In mapping out the Weberian roots of Austrian economics and explaining the full connection between Weber's interpretative sociology and Mises' praxeology, Boettke (1998b) notes that the strength of the Weber-Austrian approach to social theory was its tendency to neither oversocialize nor undersocialize people. "Individuals," Boettke (1998b: 68) asserts, "are not assumed to maximize within an institutionless vacuum, nor are they assumed to be merely puppets of structural forces beyond their control." And, as Boettke and Storr (2002: 168) claim, the individual for Weber and the

Austrians is "tri-embedded" in the economy, the polity, and the society, not a caricature only situated in either one of three.

In order to fully understand tri-embedded economic actors situated in various cultural-historical circumstances, Weber advocated a focus on the economic "spirits" that animated markets. In *The Protestant Ethic and the "Spirit" of Capitalism* (2002 [1905]), Weber claimed that capitalism can actually look different across time and place, that is, capitalism can take on various forms. He also claimed that the particular form of capitalism that took root in a given time or place would be animated by a particular ethic or spirit. A spirit or ethic of capitalism was a set of conventionally held principles for moral behavior, messages about how people were to behave and what sorts of actions constituted the highest good. In Weber's analyses, religion was typically the primary force animating people with a particular capitalist ethic or spirit. Furthermore, while it was possible for a society's spirit of capitalism and its form of capitalism to not complement each other, Weber argued that "the capitalistic 'form' of an economy and the spirit in which it is run do indeed stand in a generally *adequate* relationship to each other" (2002 [1905]: 19).

Weber examined the capitalist economies of Western Europe and the USA existing from the seventeenth century onward, describing their form of capitalism as *modern*. Weber argued that modern capitalism was animated by a *Protestant ethic*. Values held by market actors infused with the Protestant ethic included asceticism, rationality, and "tireless work in a calling" (Weber 2002 [1905]: 78). This Protestant ethic, Weber (2002 [1905]) explained, coevolved with modern capitalism, encouraging entrepreneurship and driving increases in economic growth. According to Weber (2002 [1905]: 12), this particular spirit infuses individuals with a "worldly asceticism," a compulsion to "make money and more money," a respect for the rational, scientific process toward earning money as opposed to more traditional, unscientific ones, and an ethical responsibility to engage in hard work. While Weber's results are debatable (Storr 2013: 66–70), two central claims of his project remain convincing: (a) it does appear that capitalism can take on multitude forms from society to society, and (b) each kind of capitalism present in a society is animated by a particular economic spirit or ethic.

Weber also examined *traditional* forms of capitalism, which he located in ancient and medieval economies, and those of India and China. Markets in these economies were animated by different "spirits"[3] than those in the West. For instance, under the traditionalist spirit in ancient and medieval times, the

---

[3] A "spirit" in this context refers to a society's ethos or its character; the fundamental shared values that motivate, orient, and drive people in a society as they go about their lives.

relentless pursuit of money and profit would be viewed as "an expression of the most filthy avarice and an absolutely contemptible attitude" (2002 [1905]: 14). Furthermore, Weber (1951) argued that the economic spirits of Hinduism and Confucianism encouraged adherence to various particular traditions in India and China, spirits that tended to be antithetical to the development of modern capitalism in those countries.

Since economic spirits animate economic actors and direct their economic lives, Weber argued that by investigating economic spirits, social scientists would better understand people's economic lives and the spontaneously emerging capitalist orders that they lived in. Different economic spirits offer different models of how the world works. These models give them a way to reflect on and explain the past, and to anticipate the future (Gudeman 1986). Hence, understanding these models is useful for understanding people's economic narratives, plans, and actions. In addition, economic spirits find expression not only in religious doctrines but in the everyday stories and tales passed down between generations, and the lessons imparted by them. A focus on these models and stories could therefore help social scientists understand what animates market participants in particular contexts. As Lavoie and Chamlee-Wright (2000: 53) assert, "if you want to get a sense of whether a community is apt to grow wealthier ... find out what stories they tell, what myths they believe, what heroes they admire, what metaphors they use." How people interpret and rationalize the world will influence their every decision in the economy, that is, how they produce, consume, save, invest, and so on. Hence, under the Weberian approach, social scientists interested in understanding how groups of people direct and arrange their economic lives should focus on how those groups interpret the world, and the spirits, models, and metaphors that inform their interpretation.

There are, arguably, good reasons to believe that there are often more than one economic spirit, model, or metaphor animating people in a particular context. Weber did allude to the potential existence of multiple spirits of capitalism at work in a society, asserting (2002 [1905]: 263) that, "[a]n historically given form of 'capitalism' can be filled with very different types of 'spirit,'" but he noted that a particular form of capitalism will have stronger affinities with particular types of spirit and weaker affinities with other, and he ultimately conducted his analyses by examining one spirit of capitalism per form of capitalism. Storr (2013) recommended a modification of Weber's approach to allow for the discovery of multiple economic spirits in a society. "Focusing on the dominant economic spirit that exists within a society" Storr states (2013: 69), "runs the risk of overstating the link between the dominant economic spirit in a society and that society's economic form and can obscure how competing economic spirits in a given context interact."

To paraphrase Storr's first argument, we should seek out any and all economic spirits that animate people's economic lives in a given social context, to mitigate against thinking that a society's entire economic form or set of economic arrangements must be explained with reference to an economic spirit. Multiple historical factors are often at play when theorizing about a particular form of capitalism, including political and legal facts of history. For example, modern capitalism in the USA was at least as influenced by the institution of human chattel slavery in the eighteenth and ninetieth centuries (and any spirits originating from this institution) as it was by the ethos of the English Puritans who began to migrate to New England two centuries before. Secondly, according to Storr (2013), multiple economic spirits might contradict and compete with each other (2013: 69). The interaction of clashing spirits can help to shape a society's economic form just like a uniform spirit can.

3 Non-Austrian Approaches to Exploring the Relationship between Culture and Economic Action

When non-Austrian economists study the relationship between culture and economic action, they tend to (a) view culture as reducible to norms, beliefs, and attitudes; (b) view culture as a tool, that is, as a form of capital; and/or (c) view culture as a quantitative and comparative effort.

When non-Austrian economists discuss the relationship between culture and economic action, they are typically more narrowly focused on norms, beliefs, or attitudes. This is in part because culture *qua* culture is viewed as too nebulous a concept (Guiso et al. 2006)[4] to gain analytical traction. In such a perspective, there is a supposed need to focus on proxies for culture or some of its constituent parts. One popular approach is to examine how trust in particular impacts economic outcomes (Knack and Keefer 1997, Knack and Zak 2001, Guiso et al. 2004, 2009, Tabellini 2010: 683, Algan and Cahuc

---

[4] As Guiso et al. (2006: 23) stated,

> Until recently, economists have been reluctant to rely on culture as a possible determinant of economic phenomena. Much of this reluctance stems from the very notion of culture: it is so broad and the channels through which it can enter economic discourse so ubiquitous (and vague) that it is difficult to design testable, refutable hypotheses. Without testable hypotheses, however, there is no role for culture in economics except perhaps as a selection mechanism among multiple equilibria.

The authors offer this solution: "A necessary first step is to define culture in a sufficiently narrow way, so that it becomes easier to identify a causal link from culture to economic outcomes" (2006: 23).

2010; Aghion et al. 2010).[5] Other studies look at classes of beliefs (e.g., collectivist versus individualist) or measures of various morality across cultures. These non-Austrian economists who explore the relationship between culture and economic action, in effect, treat culture as if it was a set of tools. On this view, culture is a means to help people achieve their various economic ends. Those economists who conceive of culture as a set of tools frequently survey various countries to see what particular cultural tools members of those countries possess and to what extent they have these tools. Cultural tools can be particular beliefs, values, attitudes, or norms that appear related to economic progress or stagnation. The application of these tools, it is believed, can either facilitate or hamper people's achievement of economic progress. As Storr (2013: 39) observes, "[t]he analysis typically proceeds by first identifying the set of tools that are believed to be consistent with positive economic outcomes and then linking the existence or absence of that toolkit within a particular group to that group's economic performance."

Consider, for instance, Greif's (1994) discussion of how beliefs explain the emergence and persistence of social institutions. Motivated by the question: "Why do societies fail to adopt the institutional structure of more economically successful ones?" (1994: 912), Greif found that differences in people's beliefs could explain differences in how their societies are organized, which in turn explained differences in how those societies performed economically.

Greif argued that "[c]ultural beliefs are the ideas and thoughts common to several individuals that govern interaction – between these people and between them, their gods, and other groups – and differ from knowledge in that they are not empirically discovered or analytically proved" (1994: 915). According to Greif, culture is partly comprised of beliefs, and that cultural beliefs are partly comprised of "rational cultural beliefs." Greif restricted his analysis to the latter, defining rational cultural beliefs as "beliefs that capture individual's expectations with respect to actions that others will take in various contingencies" (1994: 915). Greif posited that people develop expectations of others' actions in certain future scenarios (based on their prior experiences in the world), beliefs that guide them in *strategic* interactions.[6] Furthermore, according to Greif,

---

[5] As Tabellini (2008) describes: "To measure trust we consider the following question in the survey: 'Generally speaking, would you say that most people can be trusted or that you can't be too careful in dealing with people?' The level of trust in each region is measured by the percentage of respondents who answer that 'Most people can be trusted' (the other possible answers are 'Can't be too careful' and 'Don't know'). This variable is called trust."

[6] Although Greif in the article referenced here boils culture down to a set of specific beliefs and attitudes, Greif's broader view of culture more resembles the Austrian approach we expand on later. In particular, Greif carefully considers the historical context influencing people's thoughts and actions, and argues that the strategies people adopt to navigate the economy are shaped by this learned orientation toward the world.

rational cultural beliefs also affect interpersonal interaction in ways that are not necessarily strategic. For example, people have "social constructs" (1994: 613) in their minds about others, constructs that are apparent in the ways that people categorize themselves and others into particular identities. People hold beliefs about what membership in these groups signify and these beliefs can dictate how people treat each other. Finally, Greif points out that when people enforce moral codes, they transform their beliefs into values. Hence, cultural beliefs can also influence values.

Greif compared the cultural beliefs and social organization of the Jewish Maghribi traders of the eleventh century to those of the Latin Genoese traders of the twelfth century. Although they were Jewish and not Muslim, the Maghribi people of North Africa took up the values of Muslim society (1994: 922). Greif claimed that the Maghribi traders held *collectivist* attitudes, given their adherence to an Islamic belief that persons in their society originated from the same nation/mother as well as an Islamic belief suggesting that they each had a responsibility to keep each other from sin (1994: 922). The Maghribis similarly adhered to a Jewish belief in mutual responsibility. Meanwhile, the Genoese demonstrated *individualistic* attitudes. Theirs was a Christian society, where one's salvation was believed to be a purely personal matter, and not a matter of concern to the rest of the group.

Stemming from these beliefs (as well as other socioeconomic particularities of the two societies), the Maghribis and Genoese acted differently in their strategic trading interactions. Traders from both groups had to decide whether to travel overseas to engage with foreign traders themselves, or whether they could trust agents to act on their behalf in overseas trade. Collectivist Maghribi merchants hired agents from within their own merchant group, created business partnerships among friends and family, shared information about each other through letters and gossip, and shunned cheating merchants and agents collectively. On the other hand, the more individualist Genoese conducted trade much more impersonally. They hired agents from both inside and outside of their merchant group and their larger social group. The Genoese, therefore, had to develop formal mechanisms of verifying the trustworthiness of agents in order to advance their trade. As a result, Greif argued, the Genoese developed a society that was economically hierarchical, with more ability for upward mobility, and which laid the institutional foundation for impersonal trade among large and disparate groups of people. The collectivist Maghribi society, with its flat structure and reliance on close, informal networks for information sharing, did not develop similar institutions and hence did not over time perform economically as well as the Genoese.

Several studies have explored how other "cultural" values and beliefs, such as a group's collectivist or individualist beliefs, affect that group's progress. Aoki et al. (2012: 228), for instance, argue that individualist societies will experience more innovation and hence more growth, because the pressure to conform is much less than in collectivist societies. They also argue that individualist societies will display more "progress-prone" values in general. Such values include a respect for individual property rights and an openness and willingness to trade with foreigners and let them in. Other values associated with individualism include a dependence on formal law for conflict resolution and a desire to impose constraints on a government that is expected to be untrustworthy in the absence of those constraints. Finally, the authors argue that individualist societies will hold a high respect for values like freedom, equality, and fraternity.

Gorodnichenko and Roland (2017) sought to demonstrate that economic growth is greater in nations where people are more culturally individualist, and smaller among collectivist peoples. They proposed that individualist/collectivist traits should be the salient cultural variable impacting the economic performance of nations, since "cross-cultural psychologists consider the individualism-collectivism distinction to be the main dimension of cultural variation" (2017: 402). The authors defined culture as "the set of values and beliefs people have about how the world (both nature and society) works, as well as the norms of behavior derived from that set of values." They hypothesized that innovators would flourish in a society of people who valued individualism and behaved as such, since individualism "awards social status to personal accomplishments such as important discoveries, innovations, great artistic or humanitarian achievements, and all actions that make an individual stand out" (2017: 402). In contrast, innovation would happen only incrementally in collectivist societies, where people are rewarded more for fitting in than for standing out. Since individualism breeds the type of innovation that leads to economic growth, individualist societies would, they argued, have higher economic growth.

The authors obtained measures of individualism using Hofstede's individualism index (2001). This index is constructed using answers from national surveys that ask respondents a variety of questions meant to, among other things, measure the degree to which people want their work to accord them personal freedom, creative problem-solving, fulfillment, advancement, and personal recognition, as opposed to harmony and cooperation with their colleagues and bosses. Nations where persons surveyed tend to value the former set of criteria are given a higher score on the individualism index. Gorodnichenko and Roland (2017) employ an instrumental variable strategy to demonstrate that countries with higher individualism scores (like the UK and USA) have higher incomes and generate more patents per million persons than countries that are more collectivist (like Pakistan and Ghana).

Similar to Greif, Tabellini (2008: 256) asked "what is the mechanism through which distant political and economic history shapes the functioning of current institutions?" Like Greif, Tabellini tried to explain why certain countries remained economically underdeveloped relative to others. He asserted that redistributive conflicts and economic incentives were insufficient obstructions to the improvement of political institutions. Instead, Tabellini's (2008: 258–259) simple hypothesis was that the past influences the future through culture. Specifically, he argued that "culture may be an important channel through which distant history influences current institutional outcomes." A society that espoused a culture of "generalized morality" was a society where people valued the notion of basic individual rights and the universal equality of all people. People in such a society would apply norms of good conduct in a society toward all others, regardless of the group to which they belonged. In a society characterized by a culture of "limited morality," however, only the clan or kin network would be treated according to norms of good conduct. For persons from all other groups, "opportunistic and highly selfish behavior is regarded as natural and morally acceptable" (2008: 260). Tabellini proposed that societies would be more likely to develop a culture of generalized morality once they had a history of non-despotic institutions. Furthermore, an existing culture of generalized morality would explain the persistence of good political institutions into the present time.

Tabellini understood culture as "a set of principles and normative values that motivate individuals" (2008: 259), "transmitted vertically from one generation to the next" in a manner that is "slow and conservative" (2008: 260). He posited that how people acted in political processes would be affected by their normative values, their "conceptions of what is right or wrong, and how one ought to behave in specific circumstances" (2008: 257). For the purpose of his analysis, Tabellini restricted the scope of relevant normative values to trust and respect for others. Wherever people valued the extension of trust and respect to all others in their society, Tabellini argued, laws would be easier to enforce, bureaucracies would be less corrupt, and voters would keep politicians accountable for upholding the general social welfare as opposed to the benefit of particular people or groups that these voters preferred. "Better values are a source of comparative advantage," Tabellini asserted (2008: 289), because wherever people exhibited a generalized morality in their attitudes toward others, good governance would arise and economic exchange would flourish. In addition to trust and respect for others, Tabellini, like Greif, felt that another important and related component of culture was individualist versus collectivist attitudes. Tabellini posited that someone from an individualistic culture would be more likely to respect the rights of abstract individuals, whereas a collectivist attitude would privilege the rights of some over others.

Tabellini turned to the World Values Survey in order to measure people's cultural attitudes toward others – specifically, trust in others and respect for others. Tabellini found that the presence of high-quality political institutions in a country's past (e.g., strong constraints on executive power) had a positive influence on levels of trust and respect toward all others in the society. He also found that low corruption, high bureaucratic quality, greater tax compliance, and better property rights protection were more likely to be found in countries where levels of trust and respect for others were high. Finally, Tabellini observed that output per capita was higher in places with higher levels of trust and respect for others. As a result, Tabellini concluded that variations in governance and in economic performance could be explained by differences in trust and respect.

Several other studies have focused on the relationship between quantified survey measures of trust and economic growth. Knack and Keefer (1997: 1252), for instance, describe how trust might possibly impact economic progress. "Individuals in higher-trust societies," they (Knack and Keefer 1997) argue,

> can spend less to protect themselves from being exploited in economic transactions. Written contracts are less likely to be needed, and they do not have to specify every possible contingency. Individuals in high-trust societies are also likely to divert fewer resources to protecting themselves – through tax payments, bribes, or private security services and equipment – from unlawful (criminal) violations of their property rights. Low trust can also discourage innovation: if entrepreneurs must devote more time to monitoring possible malfeasance by partners, employees, and suppliers, they have less time to devote to innovation in new products or processes.

Culture, on this account, influences trust, which, in turn, influences transaction costs. High trust cultures have lower transaction costs and, therefore, experience more beneficial economic activity relative to low trust cultures.

Guiso et al. (2006: 23) define culture as "those customary beliefs and values that ethnic, religious, and social groups transmit fairly unchanged from generation to generation." They endeavor to show first how people's beliefs and preferences might derive from cultural transmission, and second how these culturally formed beliefs and preferences translate into economic outcomes. Using the General Social Survey to examine specific beliefs involving trust among Americans of various ethnic origins, they observe that "the level of trust an American has toward others depends in part upon where ancestors originated" (2006: 31). They find that Americans from more trusting ethnic backgrounds are more likely to become entrepreneurs, positing that "trust-worthy individuals will have a comparative advantage in becoming entrepreneurs" (2006: 35). The authors, therefore, argue that there is a causal link between cultural beliefs and an important economic outcome – entrepreneurship.

In addition to beliefs, Guiso et al. (2006) discuss their work examining cultural preferences. They observe that one's religious background can shape one's preferences over saving and thrift. Specifically, they find that Catholics, Protestants, Buddhists, Hindus, and Jewish people are all more likely than nonreligious people to teach their children about the importance of saving and thrift. They also find that national savings rates correlate positively with the proportion of people within a country that prefer thrift, suggesting again that cultural preferences affect critical economic outcomes.

Guiso et al. (2009) isolated attitudes toward trust as the key cultural factor that influenced whether people of different nationalities will engage in economic exchange. Examining survey respondents from nations within Europe, they found that wherever trust was high between European nations, those nations exhibited a high degree of international trade and investment with each other, relative to nations to where trust was low.[7] As an illustration, their data showed that "the British perception of the trustworthiness of the Dutch and French makes the British trade 30% more with the former than with the latter" (2009: 1129). Positing that culturally similar groups trust each other more than groups that are culturally distinct from one another, the authors sought to ascertain factors that made groups culturally similar in the first place. They found that cultural similarity and hence trust increases when groups share a common religion, close "genetic distance," close somatic distance (their people are similar in physical appearance), and when their ancestors have been on the same side of a war.

Harrison and Huntington (2000) also use the World Values Survey to isolate values and beliefs that are theorized to be positively correlated with progress. As argued in that volume, "the value systems of richer countries differ systematically from those of poorer countries" (2000: 88). They find that countries with Protestant values, like Germany, Switzerland, and the Netherlands, outperform countries with Catholic values, like Spain, Italy, and those comprising Latin America.

---

[7] Survey participants were asked "I would like to ask you a question about how much trust you have in people from various countries. For each, please tell me whether you have a lot of trust, some trust, not very much trust, or no trust at all" (Guiso et al. 2009: 1100).

Fernández and Fogli (2009) also examine what they call "the quantitative impact of culture" (175), finding that married women who were born in the USA to parents who immigrated from a subset of nine particular countries demonstrated similar labor force participation rates and fertility rates as representative women from their parents' country of origin a generation before.[8] The authors see culture "as systematic differences in preferences and beliefs across either socially or geographically differentiated groups" (2009: 147). They posit that, despite strong tendencies toward assimilation to the culture of the USA a woman's choices about whether and how much to work "may depend on how she perceives the role of women in the household, her beliefs as to whether children benefit or are harmed by having a working mother, preferences over market and household work, and expectations as to how she would be treated by her local society (e.g., her neighbors) as a result of working or not, etc." (2009: 148).

Mathers and Williamson (2011: 235), likewise, put the spotlight on "economic culture," which they defined as "specific indicators of culture that are identified as being relevant for supporting the capitalist foundation of economic interaction and exchange." Mathers and Williamson considered whether particular cultural "components" could make capitalism work better. If so, they posited, then groups whose cultures contained these components would perform better economically, conditional on having capitalist institutions like private property, rule of law, and contract enforcement that are objectively meant to promote economic exchange and entrepreneurship.

Mathers and Williamson hypothesized that these capitalist institutions would have more "legitimacy," that is, be more acceptable and more valuable among groups of people whose cultures contained the following four components: trust, respect, self-determination, and disobedience (2011: 235). First, an economy would exhibit greater levels of trade and profit-oriented behavior wherever its people possessed high levels of trust in each other, since trust in others makes trade with others easier. Second, mutually honest and fair exchanges are also more likely to occur among people who tolerate and respect each other's rights, even if they are strangers to one another. Hence, respect for others also promotes capitalism. Third, capitalism would thrive among a group of people who had self-determination within their culture, since entrepreneurship, the engine of economic progress, is more likely to be pursued among people who believe their personal efforts and hard work can bring them success. Finally, people would be

---

[8] Specifically, they find that: "A one standard deviation increase in LFP (labor force participation) in 1950 is associated with an approximately 7.5 percent increase in hours worked per week in 1970. A one standard deviation increase in TFR (total fertility rate) in 1950 is associated with approximately 0.4 extra children, a 14 percent increase in the number of children in 1970" (Fernández and Fogli 2009: 149).

more likely to act on entrepreneurial opportunities if obedience is not a feature of their culture. This is because entrepreneurial decision-making requires autonomy and risk-taking more than it requires compliance and acquiescence.

Mathers and Williamson found that capitalist societies with the right economic cultures did grow faster. Regressing GDP growth on the product of (i) a country's level of economic freedom (as measured by the country's Economic Freedom of the World Index score) and (ii) a country's economic culture (as measured by an index reflecting a composite of answers from the World Values Survey that pertain to trust, respect for others, self-determination, and obedience), the authors found that "culture enhances freedom's impact on growth by approximately 10 percentage points," which implies that "countries with informal institutions in line with the economic institutions captured by the freedom index will experience a higher rate of return from such institutions" (2011: 241). They conclude that culture is "the 'informal glue' that contributes to creating binding constraints, enhancing the overall effectiveness of economic institutions" (2011: 241). The use of the "glue" metaphor here suggests that culture serves to assist its users with exchange, entrepreneurship, and ultimately economic progress. Seeing culture as a set of tools suggests that culture gets applied toward the fulfillment of people's goals related to economic production, and that those who have better cultural tools will be more productive.

Alesina and Giuliano (2015) present an extensive set of summaries of economic research that examine the impact of culture on institutions and vice versa. The authors took care to differentiate each concept, pointing out that economists tend to define culture as values/preferences or beliefs (2015: 901), but sometimes also define culture as informal institutions – norms and conventions (2015: 902). They surveyed the most studied cultural variables in economics, naming these as trust, generalized morality, individualism versus collectivism, family ties, and attitudes toward work. Furthermore, the authors traced the many mechanisms by which culture has been posited to affect a variety of formal institutions (including financial, legal, and political), and mechanisms by which formal institutions have shaped culture.

Indeed, culture and institutions have also been demonstrated to interact, coevolve, and complement one another. For instance, Alesina and Giuliano (2015: 932) cite work by Alesina et al. (2015), showing that "[a]n inherited culture of strong family ties leads to a preference for labor-market rigidity; the latter, in turn, makes it optimal to teach and adopt strong family ties." The idea is that when people value living geographically closer to their families, they may agitate politically for particular formal labor institutions (like high minimum wages and strict rules against firing employees) in order to prevent companies from taking advantage of their culturally imposed geographic immobility. As such institutions cause rigidities in the labor market, unemployment may rise, which further requires families to strengthen their ties and their ability to live together. Hence, culture and institutions can impact each other in ways that may enhance each other's effects.

Additionally, there have been several experimental studies that have looked at how culture impacts how individuals perform in trust, ultimatum, and public choice games (Roth et al. 1991, Weimann 1994, Burlando and Hey 1997, Hemesath and Pomponio 1998, Ockenfels and Weimann 1999, Fan 2000, Henrich 2000, Henrich et al. 2001, Buchan et al. 2004, Carpenter et al. 2004, Holm and Danielson 2005). Roth et al. (1991), for instance, found that there were statistically significant differences in the offers made by US, Japanese, and Israeli subjects in ultimatum games. Similarly, Henrich (2000) found that cultural differences appear to affect economic behavior. Henrich (2000) compared Machiguenga and Los Angeles subjects and found that Los Angeles subjects proposed significantly higher offers than Machiguenga subjects. Chuah et al. (2007), likewise, found that Malaysian Chinese subjects offered more as proposers in ultimatum games when interacting with other Malaysian subjects than UK subjects proposed when interacting with other UK subjects. They also found that Malaysian subjects made higher offers to members of their own groups than did to UK subjects.

These studies demonstrate that economists studying culture tend to approach culture from a similar perspective and using similar frameworks and techniques. In contrast to the Austrian approach, which will be presented later, these economists tend to define culture as beliefs, attitudes, or norms. These are treated as tools or capital that groups can possess, where groups in possession of "good" tools (like individualist attitudes and a belief in the trustworthiness of others) see their economic performance enhanced, while groups with "bad" tools perform worse on economic measures (like income and working hours). Finally, all of the studies measure culture quantitatively using proxies, in order to facilitate cross-country comparison.

The next section highlights the distinctive features of the Austrian approach to exploring the relationship between culture and economic action.

4 Unique Features of the Austrian Approach to Studying the Relationship between Culture and Economic Action

The Austrian approach to studying the relationship between culture and economic action differs in important respects from non-Austrian efforts. First, Austrians view economics as a science of meaning and so focus on culture as a source meaning rather than focusing on culture as specific norms, beliefs, and attitudes. Second, Austrians tend to view culture more as an interpretive lens and less as a tool. Third, Austrians insist that cultural analysis must be a qualitative exercise rather than a quantitative effort.

4.1 Economics as a Science of Meaning and Culture as Meaning

Hayek (1948) has argued convincingly that the facts of the social sciences are what people believe and think. The fundamental data that concerns social science, as opposed to the physical sciences, are not the physical properties of objects or actions per se, but rather, people's thoughts and feelings about various aspects of the world. As Hayek (1948: 60) argues, "in the social sciences the things are what people think they are. Money is money, a word is a word, a cosmetic is a cosmetic, if and because somebody thinks they are."[9] Elaborating on Hayek's example, small metal disks and green pieces of paper with particular markings on them are not money in essence. That a person cannot simply make metal disks or cut pieces of paper, put markings on them, and then expect others to accept those objects as new legal tender is evidence that the concept of money is something wholly different from the physical properties of the objects that are accepted as money. That a person cannot simply invent a particular arrangement of sounds and letters and expect others to adopt that arrangement for communication is further evidence that the concept of language is something wholly different from a pattern of sounds and letters. The concepts that we attach to various physical objects or to various utterances are but concepts – they exist in the minds of people.

Hayek argues that this categorical distinction between conceptions about objects and the physical properties of those same objects is what separates social scientific phenomena from physical scientific phenomena. This distinction raises two important points for the orientation of an economic researcher. For one, the act of engaging in social science requires a focus on the relevant subjects' beliefs and thoughts. Where social scientists are preoccupied with categorizing a human phenomenon by its physically observable properties – for example, the *number* of certain people employed somewhere, the *distribution* of

---

[9] Knight (1925: 262) believed similarly, arguing that social scientists "are at least as much concerned with what others feel and think as with what they do in a physical sense." Like Hayek after him, Knight (1925: 256) challenged his contemporaries' belief that to be understood, human behavior need only be reduced to its physical properties,

> Does a human being really do as he does merely because he is an organism 'set' to make that response to that physical situation, as a gun loaded and cocked goes off when the trigger is pulled, or do we feel sure that there is more to the matter, that the 'situation' has 'meanings' for the 'organism' while the latter has 'attitudes' toward the situation, which are ultimately more than configuration and movement of something (or of nothing, as the logic of physics seems to indicate)?

payments among persons, or the *color* of someone's skin – then the social scientists' focus is fundamentally misplaced, if Hayek is to be believed. Rather, people's actual beliefs and thoughts about employment, income, and skin color (staying with the previous examples) are the true data that the social scientist must interrogate. As Knight (1925: 265) argued, "we can learn more by studying the ways in which *minds* know and influence each other than we ever can by attempting to analyze mechanically the process of interaction between bodies". For Knight and Hayek then, the social scientist must therefore view these data – people's thoughts and feelings – as the ultimate data to be acquired and understood.

Second and relatedly, the social scientist will not always be able to successfully ascribe their conceptions about phenomena to their subjects, as it is possible that the subjects may have different beliefs and thoughts about the phenomena than the researcher. In keeping with Hayek's example, a researcher cannot expect that because they know of some people who conceptualize particular metal disks as money, that these metal disks constitute money in a universal sense. Money is not money because the social scientist has declared it as money. Rather, money may be money if the scientist has investigated the beliefs and thoughts of the subjects in question through some appropriate method, and has discovered that the subjects equate a certain object or set of actions with the concept of a currency. As Mises (1949: 26) has said, "we may call the offering of a commodity for sale a 'stimulus'. But what is essential in such an offer and what distinguishes it from other offers cannot be described without entering into the meaning which the acting parties attribute to the situation." In sum, social scientists have to seek out the meanings that subjects already attach to their world and cannot invent or assume these meanings. The meanings that people bring with them in their interactions with the world and as they navigate it – what people think things are and how they feel about them – must take primacy.

If Hayek is right, then social sciences in general and Austrian economics by extension are sciences of subjective phenomena. If we can distinguish the subjective "characteristics" of a phenomenon – the beliefs and thoughts people hold about it – from its objective characteristics, then the distinctiveness of the social sciences is that they concern themselves with the former. So central are these subjective characteristics of phenomena to the Austrian understanding of social science that Hayek (1952: 31) conjectured "it is probably no exaggeration to say that every important advance in economic theory during the last hundred years was a further step in the consistent application of subjectivism." Hayek was referring in part to economists' eventual insistence that economic "goods" were defined as things that people wanted, irrespective of the physical nature of the things in question, and irrespective of whatever characteristics of those things economists thought mattered. People's subjective assessments of things is what economic science is about at its core.

Stated another way, social science and economics are about meaning. Hence, Austrian economics is a science of meaning. Austrian economists have been particularly self-aware that the goal of a science of subjective phenomena is to capture the meanings that our subjects themselves attach to their world, and Austrian economists concerned with methodology have taken care to explain why economics is a science of meaning that should concern itself with the meanings that economic actors attach to the world as they make their decisions. As Mises (1949: 26) put it, "we cannot approach our subject if we disregard the meaning which acting man attaches to the situation, i.e. the given state of affairs, and to his own behavior with regard to this situation." Hayek (1952: 53) also reiterated that "unless we can understand what . . . people mean by their actions any attempt to explain them . . . is bound to fail."

Austrian economics endorses the requirement for economists to pay attention to their subjects' opinions about the subjects' own experiences. The ultimate significance of a thing under study is not for the economist to determine by appealing to the physical properties of the thing, but by observing the relevant subjects' opinions, assessments, and valuations of it. To elucidate this point, Knight (1925) argued that even an illusion is an example of a social scientific phenomena. Knight argued that a scientist can only claim that a subject's perception of something is an illusion by observing some other relevant subjects' claim to existence of an illusion, and not by the researcher's reliance on their own physical sense perceptions. In other words, what the researcher can or cannot see is moot. As Knight argues (1925: 252): "The 'snakes' seen by the sufferer from delirium tremens are doubtless as 'real' . . . as those of the jungle or the museum, but they are 'unreal' *because others do not see them*" (italics ours). Thus, the first relevant fact for the researcher is the original subject's belief that she sees a snake. And, if others in the original subject's group think that she is under an illusion that a snake is present, then the group members' denial of the snake's existence is another relevant social scientific fact. An alternative possibility the researcher might encounter is that the others know that they do not see a snake, yet they believe the original subject can see a snake that they cannot see. In that case, group members would not think that a member of their group is experiencing an illusion but rather that they have preternatural perception. According to Knight, only in people's minds do distinctions exist between reality and illusion, truth and falsity, importance and frippery, tradition and logic, and so on. In interrogating beauty in a society, for example, it would be unscientific for the researcher to go about measuring physical attributes like objective height or weight to assess beauty. Instead, facts about beauty are what the relevant subjects believe and think are beautiful – their subjective assessments of what things are and are not beautiful. Only by uncovering these various meanings can the economist make advances in understanding those people.

Since Austrian economics is a science fundamentally concerned with meaning, the concept of meaning deserves some unpacking. Meaning is a simply a way of seeing. For Schütz (1967: 42), "meaning is a certain way of directing one's gaze at an item of one's own experience." To say that people act is to say that people attribute meaning to what they do, that is, that people act in the service of a particular goal, where the goal exists in the mind of the actor. A surgical procedure, for example, is not a robotic response to stimuli, but is instead an act carried out in the service of some broad set of personal and subjective goals, including the surgeon's desire to make the patient better, the surgeon's belief that conducting the procedure will support or improve the surgeon's lifestyle, the surgeon's belief that doing the procedure will fulfill the surgeon's family's dreams, and so on. Crucially, declaring that the surgeon is acting hinges upon a recognition than the surgeon has goals or end states for themselves or others in mind before they conducts the procedure. Thus, actions, as Schütz (1967: 26) says, "are meaningless apart from the project that defines it." The surgical procedure has meaning because, for one, the surgeon sees the procedure in particular ways.

Although meanings are paramount in the social world, as meanings are essentially intangible data of the mind, the social scientist does not literally have access to the meanings that subjects attribute to the world. Problematizing the fundamental inaccessibility of meanings, Schütz (1967) distinguishes between two levels of meaning behind every action – the "in-order-to motive" that influences an action, and the true "because-of motive" behind that action. To clarify this distinction, the surgeon in our previous example may believe that they are going through with a procedure *in order to* heal the patient, but why do they actually see the world that way? Where does the belief about the efficacy of this particular procedure ultimately come from, and why do they subscribe to it? According to Schütz, while we cannot get the answer in an ultimate and essential sense as we do not have God-like access to people minds, we can still attempt to grasp why things mean what they mean to people. For one, social scientists are people themselves. Hence, they have the ability to interpret what other people do. Furthermore, Schütz argues that once we interrogate a subject's social stock of knowledge, we can approximate the subject's motives. As Storr (2013: 28) describes it,

> An individual's 'subjective stock of knowledge' contains everything that he
> has 'learned' over the course of his life; how to walk, talk, read, ride a bicycle,
> drive a car, relate to his friends and colleagues, program a computer, reason
> like an economist; what his capabilities are and his limitations; what is
> appropriate and inappropriate in a variety of the circumstances; what is
> typically relevant and what is usually irrelevant in various situations; which
> phenomena he should view as common and which uncommon; his own life
> history; the stories he was told as a child; what he gained through interacting
> with this fellows; the customs and folklore of his community. When an event
> occurs or he is confronted with a (novel or not so novel) state of affairs, he
> draws on his subjective stock of knowledge as he defines his circumstances
> and decides his path.

There are, arguably, various links between what Schütz calls the "social stock of knowledge" and the concept of culture as put forward by Geertz (1973) and adopted by the Austrians. This implies that in order to get at the meanings motivating people's actions, the social scientist must try to understand people's culture.

This means that Austrian economics is at its core a cultural discipline. Understanding what apples *mean* to a group of people, for instance, is essential if we are to understand how and why they react as they do to a change in the price of apples. Presumably, wherever the eating of apples is culturally prohibited, or wherever the eating of apples is culturally required, small changes in the price of apples is unlikely to significantly affect the group's consumption of apples. Without referencing culture, that is, without understanding the ethos and worldview of the groups in question, it would be impossible in these scenarios to understand why these groups of people have a relatively inelastic demand for apples. Although we cannot literally get inside other people's brains, as social scientists, we have to attempt to interpret their actions, and to uncover the meanings behind those actions. In other words, we must engage in cultural study.

Austrian economics takes the requirement of economists to engage in cultural study to be ineluctable. Thus, the researcher can reference or engage with their subjects' culture reference either implicitly or explicitly, but culture can never actually be avoided (Storr 2013). As the apples example shows, when an economist tells a story about relative price changes, the economist may or may not take it as given that apples have a particular significance to the subjects in question. Apples have subjective characteristics, which is to say that people have particular beliefs and thoughts about apples that derive from their social stock of knowledge. The subjects' apple buying/selling actions presumes meaning about apples, that they regard apples in a particular way. The economist can choose to leave these meanings explicit, or not. But the point remains that why and how a person signifies apples as a good, surgery as a career choice, or the use of metal disks as currency depends on what's in that person's social stock of knowledge, their culture. Culture can, therefore, be in the background or fore-ground of an economic analysis of people buying or selling apples, performing surgery, or using money, but culture is always there, a part of every economic story.

Often, the best economic stories are those in which culture is in the fore-ground of the analysis, and in which the researcher has endeavored to examine their subjects' culture in order to interpret their subject's actions. Because, as previously mentioned, subjects may hold different beliefs and thoughts about phenomena than the researcher does, the researcher might come away with interpretations of subjects' actions that are closer to the subjects' true motives in economic decision-making if the researcher examines the subjects' culture explicitly. Lavoie and Chamlee-Wright (2000), for instance, advocate bringing culture to the fore in the examination of economic decision-making. They argue that the study of enterprise is fundamentally a cultural project, and that examin-ing the culture behind entrepreneurial decisions enhances the economic under-standing of markets. For one, they contend that "cultural studies can explicitly show how limited the narrower instrumental sense of self-interestedness is, and demonstrate by solid ethnographic work the complex interconnectedness and interdependence of individuals in society" (2000: 41). Lavoie and Chamlee-Wright thus argue for a new cultural reading of business, which demonstrates the various moral and social factors, the beliefs and values that drive the interactions of entrepreneurs, workers, and consumers. Additionally, Lavoie and Chamlee-Wright (2000: 48) support the exploration of the various cultural factors underpinning non-Western economies, stating that "[t]he complex domestic markets of African, Latin America, and Asia have well-established roots in the history and culture of their respective indigenous societies." Arguably then, an understanding of markets in the societies as they function requires explicit examination of their culture and history.

Since Austrian economics is a science of meaning, it must be concerned with culture if it is to uncover the in-order-to and genuine because-of motives of economic actors. Culture for Austrian economists is, thus, not reducible to norms, beliefs, and attitudes.[10] Instead, Austrians tend to think of culture as a framework of meanings or as a lens through which people process the world.

---

[10] This reflects a crucial difference in how economists conduct cultural study. Most cultural research in economics attempts to get at culture by fragmenting it and zeroing in on one specific belief, attitude, or norm within a population, as opposed to thinking of culture as a full and diverse system of meanings. Cross-cultural comparisons of these isolated beliefs, attitudes, and norms tend to avoid interrogating what the world means to the groups under study. For example,

4.2 Culture as a Lens

Economic anthropologist Clifford Geertz's (1973) definition influenced and most closely accords with the Austrian view of the relationship between culture and economic action. For Geertz, culture is "an historically transmitted pattern of meanings embodied in symbols, a system of inherited conceptions expressed in symbolic forms by means of which men communicate, perpetuate, and develop their knowledge about and attitudes toward life" (1973: 89). Thus, culture equates to shared patterns of meaning that make life navigable.

Geertz explains that a cultural system is comprised of both a worldview and an ethical system that mutually support one another. "A group's ethos," Geertz (1973: 90) explains, "is rendered intellectually reasonable by being shown to represent a way of life ideally adapted to the actual state of affairs the world view describes, while the world view is rendered emotionally convincing by being presented as an image of an actual state of affairs peculiarly well-arranged to accommodate such a way of life." Culture, therefore, is how people come up with stories about how things are, as well as stories about why things are the way that they are. Stated another way, culture is the lens through which they interpret and make sense of their actions, opportunities, and environment. Culture affects how people think things "are" and informs how people think things "should be."

Four features of Geertz's concept of culture and of cultural systems are worth illuminating. For one, culture represents a complex totality of meanings, such that culture is not irreducible to one or another particular belief or value. It would be a mistake, in Geertz's view, to reduce culture to trust or individualist/collectivist attitudes. Secondly, the set of beliefs and values that comprise a cultural system constitute a stock of knowledge that has evolved over time, and that knowledge is continuously evolving. Thirdly, stocks of knowledge do not originate outside of human beings. As Geertz puts it, "man is an animal suspended in webs of significance he himself has spun" (1973: 5). This suggests that people themselves generate the meanings they ultimately adopt – the

---

while some economic research tries to show that one group has more trust among each other than another group does, these studies rarely probe subjects to understand why their beliefs, attitudes, and norms surrounding trust are the way that they are. The researchers do not try to get at their subjects' subjective assessments of the trustworthiness of other people. They do not try to situate these thoughts and beliefs within historical context. Furthermore, cultures evidently have a diversity of beliefs, attitudes, and norms within them. As such, no one cultural component is likely to be a sufficient explanation for behavior. In order to examine the multiplicity of motives that lead to the fulfillment of the surgical procedure from our previous example, we must examine the social stock of knowledge. This examination inevitably requires a rich account of how people process their world based on what they have learned. This emphasis on conducting a full account of the social stock of knowledge is what distinguishes the Austrian approach to culture from mainstream economic approaches.

meanings do not come from a source external to people. Finally, rather than generating these meanings anew at the moment of their birth, each person over the course of their life comes to adopt the existing meanings that are taught to them through interaction with others in the community.

Arguably, to think of culture the same way that we think of a tool is misleading. A tool is an instrument or technology meant to provide a specific solution. A tool is implemented in order to enable its user to undertake a specified task more easily. With an increased application of force, or with a more sophisticated design, the tool can be more successful at helping the user to accomplish a task. Physical tools like hammers, wrenches, and levers, for example, are meant to enhance production. "Better" hammers, wrenches, and levers make us more productive. Even human capital – habits, knowledge, and skills – is defined in terms of its ability to help people achieve particular tasks, to get things done or to get them done easier. Operating a plane or taking notes in a meeting are both tasks that require the person responsible for achieving those tasks to possess various types of physical and human capital.

While tools are employed instrumentally, toward the achievement of the deliberate goals for which they were designed, arguably, the concept of culture is not sufficiently similar to the concept of a tool. Instead, as noted earlier, culture can be conceived of as the lens through which individuals see and make sense of the world. As economic anthropologist Clifford Geertz (1973: 89) has described it, culture "denotes an historically transmitted pattern of meanings embodied in symbols, a system of inherited conceptions expressed in symbolic forms by means of which men communicate, perpetuate, and develop their knowledge about and their attitudes toward life." For Geertz, human beings are raised or adopted into a complex collection of shared meanings that are represented by and through symbols and spread through processes of enculturation.

A fruitful way to explain culture is by invoking the example of a wink (Geertz 1973: 6; see Ryle 2009 [1968]: 494). A wink is a visible twitch of the eye that can convey a variety of meanings, including flirtation, conspiracy, or mockery. In order for both the winker and observer to read the same meaning into the symbol, the eye-twitch, they each must have learned how to interpret and differentiate the meanings of an eye-twitch through their prior experiences (perhaps with each other) as well as meanings derived from their culture(s). A culture is a complex collection of meanings that a group of human beings learn and share. These shared meanings include notions about how the world works and how it should work. People from different cultures have different ways of seeing the world. They interpret and evaluate the world differently.

If we accept that culture is something that makes life at all moments intelligible – something always in the background, influencing the way we take in what our senses perceive, and influencing the choices we make – we can grasp why it is not wholly accurate to conceptually treat culture as a tool. Recall that Mathers and Williamson (2011) conceived of culture as a tool when they argued that the belief that other people ought to be respected supports mutually beneficial exchange between people. The authors assert that absent the tool – the belief that others have rights to be respected – mutually beneficial exchange would be much more difficult to achieve. Culture for them, therefore, is a lever that bolsters specific activities – in this case, market transactions. However, Geertz (1973) cautions against the temptation to reduce culture to instrumental behavior. As he says, "culture is best seen not as complexes of concrete behavior patterns – customs, usages, traditions, habit clusters ... but as a set of control mechanisms – plans, recipes, rules, instructions ... for the governing of behavior" (1973: 44). For Geertz (1973: 45), man develops and shares patterns of meanings "to put a construction upon the events through which he lives, to orient himself within 'the ongoing course of experiences things.'" In the absence of culture, Geertz argued, human beings would have nothing to direct or govern their behavior. That direction or instruction about how to live our lives is not coded into us at birth the way it is for other animals. Without culture, nothing happening would hold any meaning for us. People without culture, according to Geertz, would be "unworkable monstrosities with very few useful instincts, fewer recognizable sentiments, and no intellect: mental basket cases" (1973: 49). Culture, therefore, is not something we implement to make particular things go right in our lives. Arguably, we do not use culture at all. Rather, culture animates us and gives us direction. This understanding of culture inspired Geertz to declare that people are "suspended in webs of significance" where the webs of significance are a metaphor for culture.

While many non-Austrian economists are drawn to the concept of culture as a tool used to achieve particular things, the relationship between culture and economic action is more complex. Action is packed with meaning. Geertz asserts that "human behavior is ... symbolic action – action which, like phonation in speech, pigment in painting, line in writing, or sonance in music – signifies" (1973: 10). Action is enmeshed in, motivated by, and conveys meaning. Therefore, when people act – whether they are winking at each other or trading goods with each other – the social scientist must try to figure what their actions signify. As Geertz advises, "[t]he thing to ask is what their import is: what it is, ridicule or challenge, irony or anger, snobbery or pride, that in their occurrence and through their agency, is getting said" (1973: 10). This approach is markedly different from the one that sees culture like a technology for getting things done.

Storr (2013) criticized the specific approach within economics that takes culture as a capital. Storr pointed out that, unlike hammers and nails, which are forms of capital, we do not take culture out of a tool kit when we need it and put it away when we it's no longer useful for the task at hand. Like language, culture is how we convey meaning, not how we get specific things accomplished. Likening culture to language, Storr quoted Gadamer who pointed out that "language is by no means simply an instrument, a tool. For it is in the nature of the tool that we master its use, which is to say we take it in hand and lay it aside when it has done its service" (1976: 52). Further, Storr critiqued the "culture as capital" approach, as it presumes that culture, like capital, may be deliberately acquired through some kind of sacrifice, and is deliberately and intentionally deployed for specific purposes. Additionally, culture is not an item in the utility function, something we prefer more of to less. Rather, culture refers to how we see the world as we go about constructing our utility functions, that is, deciding what we desire and deciding how our desires relate to one another. One final argument presented by Storr against thinking of culture as capital is that the analogy can lead to misleading comparisons of cultures. Since capital represents tools that we use to make things better, having more capital or more of a "good" capital is superior relative to having less capital. Operationalizing culture as a tool can lead to economists ultimately making assessments of the cultural "strengths" and "weaknesses" of various groups of people.[11]

We must note, however, that as the meaning of culture is contestable, so too is the analogy of culture as a tool.[12] Even among Austrian economists, culture has

---

[11] The "scoring" approach to culture takes the view that cultural capital can enhance or depress a society's economic development performance. This approach explicitly says that cultures possessing certain "good" components are inherently predisposed to economic progress, while those with a different set of components are culturally progress-resistant (Harrison 1992, 2008). For example, cultural factors deemed to be conducive to economic development include positive attitudes toward competition and work, as well as rationalist and optimist attitudes. Lavoie and Chamlee-Wright (2000) refer to this approach as "checklist ethnography" and "cultural nationalism" (2000: 62). In addition to being an offensive and politically dangerous approach, the authors point out that any so-called cultural strength could be a value or attitude that is detrimental to economic progress (or vice versa) in some other way that the economic researchers failed to notice because they did not study the context more holistically. As they argue, "The research mode here should not be to formulate a binary categorization of a culture – Is it optimistic or not? – but to qualitatively examine specific cultural advantages on their own terms. Within every society are competing definitions of economic prosperity, and each has a heterogeneous array of conflicting cultural tendencies that resist aggregation" (2000: 62). And, for Storr (2013), the astonishing fact of Caribbean slaves growing produce to sell in markets in spite of their lack of freedom suggests that "[a] definite spirit of enterprise can be found in the most unlikely places," and more strongly, that "there is no such thing as a culture that cannot develop" (2013: 4).

[12] One way to perhaps reconcile this tension is to view culture-as-lens and culture-as-tool as referring to two related but distinct concepts, and to view our project here as exploring how

been defined as both patterns of meaning and a tool. Lavoie and Chamlee-Wright, for instance, share the view that "culture is the underlying context that makes the world meaningful, that gives any particular cause meaning" (2000: 23), and, at the same time, the authors approvingly cite Mark Jacobs (1994), who asserted, "We now tend to view culture as a context rather than a force; a 'tool-kit' of habits, skills and styles from which people construct strategies of action in everyday life" (2000: 8). On this, Lavoie and Chamlee-Wright find support from Swidler (1986: 277) who explicitly envisioned culture as a "'tool-kit' or repertoire from which actors select differing pieces for constructing lines of action." Operationalizing this view of culture as a tool kit, Chamlee-Wright (2002) focused on women entrepreneurs in Zimbabwe and the specific tools or strategies the women used in order to participate in urban markets, to save and provide mutual assistance, to invest, to diversify their businesses, and to maintain control over their resources, all despite the barriers facing them. Such strategies included contributing their money to informal rotating credit organizations in which women were the only members, using their payouts from these organizations to make investments in their businesses, avoiding marriage to keep control of their business, or forming business partnerships with their husbands while maintaining business autonomy and control. These strategies, Chamlee-Wright argued, developed in response to a cultural context with specific values prevalent in Zimbabwean society and specific obstacles facing women entrepreneurs there. As another example, Chamlee-Wright and Storr (2010b) demonstrated how the residents of a Vietnamese-American community in New Orleans repeated stories of how their community historically overcame adversity in order to infuse current members of the community with the belief that they could rebuild the community in the aftermath of Hurricane Katrina. The telling of specific stories could be understood as a specific cultural tool deployed by community leaders to enact change. In short, culture can and has been interpreted as a tool by Austrian economists, that is, in a non-Geertzian fashion.

Retuning to Geertz's definition, culture for the Austrians is "a historically transmitted pattern of meanings that is shared by a group of people and learned by new members as they become a part of the group" (Storr 2013: 3). Culture in the Austrian vision might also be described as "a framework of meaning, as *aspect* of virtually any causal factor one might identify, not a separate causal

culture-as-lens is consistent with the Austrian preoccupation with developing a science of meaning, to explore how contemporary Austrians have pursued a culture-as-lens analysis, and to highlight the distinctiveness of this approach. On this view, it is unfortunate that that same word is used to mean two different things but it becomes easier to understand why we privilege culture-as-lens.

factor on its own. It is the background that provides the linguistic framework with which we understand the world around us" (Lavoie and Chamlee-Wright 2000: 14).

Recall that, in order to operationalize Geertz's conception of culture, the social scientist must try to interpret "what is getting said" by people's actions. This, arguably, privileges detailed qualitative studies of particular contexts over comparative and quantitative studies.

4.3 Cultural Economics as a Qualitative Exercise

Quantitative and comparative studies of the relationship between culture and economic action have tended to find that culture, defined as a particular set of norms, beliefs, or attitudes matters. For certain questions regarding the relationship between culture and economic actions, then, quantitative approaches seem wholly appropriate. In particular, quantitative approaches appear most appropriate in addressing questions concerning whether or not there are differences in how people within certain cultural groups or entire cultural groups perform in certain scenarios. Quantitative approaches are most appropriate where the goal is to establish whether or not differences in culture or some cultural factors can explain economic differences.

There are, however, real limits to quantitative approaches to understanding the relationship between culture and economic action. Quantitative approaches to studying culture often are quite capable at demonstrating if and when culture matters, but do not really help us to understand how culture matters for a variety of reasons. There are difficulties in both modeling and measuring culture and its effect on economic phenomena.

For one, quantitative approaches to the study of culture tend to treat culture, at least formally, as if it is a form of capital. As noted earlier, we explained how research in this vein treats culture as a kind of tool that members of some communities possess and members of other communities do not. Consequently, it enters into formal models and regression analyses in the same way that capital does. Those who possess better versions of the tool or possess more of the "good" tool (e.g., those societies where trust is "high") are more productive and effective than those who possess inferior versions of the tool or who have less of the good tool (those societies where trust is "low"). Observed differences in economic outcomes between nations are, thus, explained by referencing differences in one or a few cultural beliefs or values between those nations.

As previously argued, we do not actively pick and collect our patterns of shared meaning, or trade off or interchange those parts of them we happen to dislike or not need. We cannot abandon and discard elements of our culture as easily as we might switch from using an iPhone to an Android. We might be able to adopt the traits of the members of a particular culture, but to be truly a member of culture, individuals must be adopted by it and raised into it. As Bourdieu (1977) argues, cultures adopt people more so than the other way around. As he (Bourdieu 1977: 18) says, "agents ... are possessed by their habitus more than they possess it." Thus, in treating culture like capital, quantitative research on the relationship between culture and economics ends up treating cultures in a misguided fashion. Culture is, therefore, not enough like the concept of capital to be approached in the same way.

Another potential problem with quantitative approaches is the tendency of quantitative studies of culture to assume that cultures are homogenous. When Harrison and Huntington (2000) describe Protestant cultures as progress-resistant and Catholic cultures as progress-prone, they isolate certain "positive" traits or values in Protestantism, and do the same for the "negative" values within those cultures. It is assumed that there are no variations within culture that are meaningful.

But it is possible for cultures to have dualities – countervailing values that exist and that moderate the tendencies described. So, for instance, it is possible that China's historical underdevelopment can be explained by its lack of an individualist culture relative to Japan, for example (Levy 1962), and that the Chinese people's embrace of markets can also be explained by culture (Allison and Lin 1999, Chow 2010). Similarly, as Storr (2004) argues, contemporary Bahamians display both an "enterprising spirit," where the fundamental belief is that "success through hard work is possible even in the face of extreme obstacles," and a "cunning spirit," where actors are always seeking opportunities to get ahead by taking advantage of others. Thus, it is at least possible that if we were to looking into the Protestant culture of Germany, either using the World Values Survey or some other method, therefore, we might find a mix of heterogeneous values, including some that undermine the secularism and rationalism that is supposed to be the sine qua non of Germany's Protestant culture and its attendant economic success.

Moreover, it is possible that the same values have different effects in different contexts. Lavoie and Chamlee-Wright (2000: 61) consider the question of whether a particular value, attitude, or norm that produces positive outcomes in one environment is necessarily universally positive. As they ask,

> Is deep respect for the past necessarily a weakness of a culture – a hindrance to economic prosperity? Perhaps yes, in a culture where respecting the past means that new agricultural techniques are never explored. In another context, however, respecting the past may carve out a place of honor for those who preserve history and tradition. In such a circumstance, the productive

potential of the elderly may be more readily recognizable, for instance, as caretakers of young children.

Hence, contra Harrison and others who suggest that cultural traits like a commitment to the past are necessary progress resistant, Lavoie and Chamlee-Wright contend that the possibility at least exists that a focus on tradition can provide an avenue for economic success. Therefore, a respect for the past and for tradition is not a universal anathema.

Similarly, while scholars have argued that generalized trust is universally conducive to economic development, others have pointed out that a low or narrow *radius* of trust – a situation where people highly trust others within their own "sub-group" relative to those outside of it – can produce ambiguous economic effects (Knack 2001). As Knack (2001: 10) says, "Cooperation that is generated by trust can produce costs as well as benefits." In one context, trust may cause in-groups to form whose activities are generally public-spirited. In another context, those within the group may support each other while they act with hostility and domination toward those on the outside (Knack references the Nazi Party in 1930s Germany as an example). In this scenario, in-group trust can lead to positive effects for the in-group, but potentially negative effects for everyone else. As Pye (2000: 255) insists, "it is unscientific to try to draw up a universal list of positive and negative cultural values for economic development. What may be positive in some circumstances can be quite counterproductive under other conditions."

Related to the point of whether the values isolated in these quantitative studies are the correct ones to isolate is the issue of whether it possible to separate these factors from others forces in a society, as quantitative approaches explicitly try to do.[13] It is unclear, however, that the values expressed in a population are separate from realities there, and hence that these values can be empirically isolated from other aspects of the environment, using regression techniques or otherwise. Particularly if we believe that culture is a pattern of shared meanings, then it stands to reason that these meanings are directly related to aspects of the physical, political, economic, social, and institutional environments.

Indeed, as Chamlee-Wright and Lavoie (2000: 14) insist, "Culture is a framework of meaning, an *aspect* of virtually any casual factor one might identify, not a separate causal factor on its own." And, as Storr (2013: 16)

---

[13] Tabellini (2008: 486) chooses to study "four related but distinct measures of culture: three indicators expected to promote economic development (trust, control, respect), and one that might hurt it (obedience)." Are these values assumed to be the only ones present in particular cultures that matter for development? As Tabellini himself confesses: "This selection has some unavoidable arbitrariness in this selection. But hopefully it does not matter much."

writes, "that culture is arguably a part of every potential factor that affects economic behavior means that it is problematic to treat it as a separate causal factor." Hence, quantitative approaches that attempt to isolate so-called cultural factors, holding constant things like institutions and geography, are, in a sense, missing the point. Culture is observed in the way people understand and interact with their environments. Hence, isolating culture from aspects of the environment is an empirical strategy that prevents us from recognizing the complex trade-offs people make and the context-dependent solutions they arrive at, and lead us to make unfortunate and unfair comparisons between different groups of people and environments.

A further potential problem with quantitative approaches that treat culture as a resource is their tendency to paint cultures as static. Like stocks of capital, characterizing cultures as "high trust" and "low individualism" suggests that they are steadfast qualities of groups of people. However, the Geertzian understanding of cultures insists that cultures are never static but are dynamic and naturally evolve. Quantitative studies of culture attempt to pin contemporary disparities in wealth on differences in culture in a way that suggests that these cultures are locked into particular frameworks.

One additional problem with the quantitative studies is the fundamental question of the appropriateness of the statistics and econometric techniques economists use to get at culture. While empirical work in culture is a necessity, we must ask whether the questions on the World Values Survey, and the answers derived from them, actually measure culture. The use of aggregate statistics to measure particular beliefs and values suffers from several problems – faulty notions of the original concept, specious measurements, incomplete information, and massive exercises in interpolation to create "data."

While most economists writing about culture address these limitations, they do not abandon the methods. As an example, Knack (2001: 182) concedes that "subsequent cross-country analyses ... have relied heavily on survey-based indicators that are doubtless highly imperfect, due to translation difficulties, sampling error, and response bias, but which nevertheless produce values that are consistent with information from independent sources."

In sum, there are several limitations associated with quantitative approaches to studying the relationship between culture and economic behavior. Arguably, qualitative approaches can allow economists to avoid some of the shortcomings involved in quantitative methods, and to tell rich, thick stories about economic action.

There are advantages to deploying qualitative methods for exploring the relationships between culture and economic analysis. As Chamlee-Wright (2010, 2011) argues, economists studying culture would benefit from using qualitative methods, including archival social history, ethnography, and in-depth case studies. Chamlee-Wright (2010) maintains that sometimes, in investigating complex social problems, qualitative research compliments quantitative research. Other times, she argues, the qualitative approach is actually superior. For example, in trying to understand how persons in New Orleans' communities experienced life before and after Hurricane Katrina, the author and her team interviewed scores of people affected by the disaster. They learned from those interviews not only that some communities rebounded quickly following the disaster while others were slower to rebound, but also how community members understood the disaster, its effects and their prospects, and the recovery strategies that they pursued. Ultimately, Chamlee-Wright (2010: 24) explained that they chose to use the interview method to answer these questions because "interview subjects possessed the local knowledge that we lacked, particularly knowledge about how and why recovery processes where failing."

In attempting to explain the benefits of qualitative approaches, Chamlee-Wright (2010: 28) invites us to think of a social or cultural system as a large, complex, multidimensional, constantly evolving puzzle. Unfortunately, no one has given the puzzle-solver – the social scientist – a picture of what the whole looks like. As such, the scientist often does not know what to make of the jumbled constituent parts. Chamlee-Wright (2010) notes that a standard reaction to this complexity is to use aggregate statistics ("trust," "religiosity," "individualism," etc.) to try to understand the influence of culture in the puzzle. This strategy, she explains, is akin to looking at the puzzle from "10,000 feet up" (2010). The problem with the "aerial view" – which mirrors the dominant strategy of economists using quantitative approaches to study the role of culture in economic growth and development – is that,

> It doesn't quite make sense to ask 'which puzzle piece is most important (in explaining some complex puzzle)?' because any single puzzle piece, absent other relevant pieces, is relatively meaningless. The real trick in understanding the meaning of the puzzle is to see how clusters of critical pieces intersect and affect one another. (2010: 29)

Thus, the quantitative strategy of isolating the most important factor or factors directs us away from the critical and important relationships between the relevant factors.

Qualitative approaches offer several advantages over quantitative strategies, especially when the subject is culture, which is an aspect of other causal factors. Chamlee-Wright (2010: 29) insists that,

> Qualitative research is like stepping inside our puzzle, so that we gain the perspective of what constitutes the environment in which our 'puzzle pieces'

are operating. We can observe not only individual behavior, but the interactions between these living/interpreting/learning/expectation-forming/strategizing beings.

The puzzle-solver must literally get inside the puzzle bag, or "come down from time to time and look at our puzzle up close" (2010: 29). "Ideally," Chamlee-Wright (2010: 29) argues, "as social scientists, we would want to talk to the people we seek to understand." She maintains that, if one seeks to uncover and understand the meanings that people ascribe to their social world, and, thus, the real motivations behind their actions, talking to those people obviously outperforms introspection. Analyzing one's own mind for another's motivations is problematic. Standing outside of another person's context, we might fail to see that person's point of view. The best strategy then is to go to the person, ask him about the facts in his environment as he sees them, and ask him how he thinks and feels about them. Quantitative strategies create too much distance between the social scientist and the person under observation, making it more difficult than need be for the former to understand the latter. Interviews are also superior to surveys in this regard. Getting responses from interview subjects allows social scientists to "make sense of behavior that within our own paradigms might not make sense" (Chamlee-Wright 2010: 30).

Furthermore, the open-ended nature of interviews means that interview questions can change as new and surprising information emerges from the interviewee. The social scientist using interviews puts themselves in a position to learn maximally from the interview, as in doing so, they allow themselves to be genuinely surprised by what the interviewee has to say. On the other hand, crafting surveys requires coming up with a tight list of questions before meeting the subjects. Chamlee-Wright suggests that this requires too much introspection from the researcher, and closes off possibilities of getting at the surprising bits local and tacit knowledge that market subjects alone possess.[14] As an example, Chamlee-Wright explains how she and her team

---

[14] Starr (2014) has made a similar point. As she explains,

> In standard quantitative research, a pre-determined set of information items is collected from research subjects (e.g. respondents to surveys) or data-reporting units (e.g. companies filing quarterly financial reports, meteorological stations reporting weather data, etc.), where the only information collected is what has been pre-specified in the research instrument. Research subjects cannot question the questions they are asked, add nuances or caveats, or explain the reasoning behind their response. Instead it is assumed a priori that the researcher knows the specific informational items that played a central role in the subjects' behaviours, perceptions and/or decisions, and can compellingly hypothesize how these items interrelate. In contrast, in qualitative studies, the approach to information gathering assumes that relatively flexible discussions with research subjects are needed for gaining a full and complete set of insights into the phenomenon of interest. (2014: 240)

were expecting interview subjects to say that their biggest challenges in rebuilding their communities after Hurricane Katrina related to physical challenges like home repairs. However, they were surprised when subjects revealed that their biggest problems actually related to the uncertainty of dealing with various bureaucracies. "By entering the field," she argues, "we gained critical insight into a central challenge of the post-disaster environment that, because it was manifest in an intangible form (e.g. confusion, postponement of action, uncertainty), might otherwise have remained hidden from view" (2010: 33).

Utilizing qualitative strategies to study how culture impacts economic behavior, therefore, allows economists to engage in a science of meaning.[15] Only by using qualitative methods like interviews, archival history, and ethnography is it possible to begin to get at the true data we want in social science, which is people's subjective assessments of what's important to them and what's meaningful to them. The closer we get to the people under our observation (while maintaining the limits required of professional scholars), the better chance we have at interpreting the experiences of others.

In sum, quantitative and qualitative methods in economics address different sorts of questions about culture. In general, quantitative cultural work *quantifies* culture in order to address questions that demand statistical answers. Quantitative cultural work seeks to determine which societies have more or less of whichever type of cultural capital the researcher believes to be necessary for economic growth. To enable static comparisons, quantitative cultural work must treat cultures as if they are frozen and uniform, that is, as if the people within the society have unchanging norms, attitudes, and beliefs, and where none of these norms, attitudes, or beliefs conflict or compete with each other. Furthermore, quantitative cultural work strips culture away from other elements of society (like political, legal, technological, and other factors), and asks how culture *as an isolated factor* bears down on people's choices.

On the other hand, qualitative methods are deployed when the researcher wants to capture descriptions of meanings, believing that meanings reflect culture. The culture researcher will talk with the subject about the subject's thoughts and beliefs about a particular situation, believing that the subject can genuinely educate them, and respecting the subject's narratives about their life experiences. Qualitative cultural research searches for complexities and dualisms in the meanings people ascribe to the world, and considers how these meanings influence people's choices across various domains of their lives. This

---

[15] Another benefit of using qualitative approaches to study culture is that it enables economists to treat the market as a cultural phenomenon, and to uncover the particular ideal typical entrepreneurs that populate and animate particular markets.

mode of research looks into a people's history for sources of cultural diversity and cultural evolution.

5 Studying Culture in the Austrian Tradition

There have been numerous studies exploring the relationship between culture and economic action by Austrian economists.

Boettke et al. (2008) shed light on how culture matters for development. They demonstrate that understanding a society's history is the key to understanding its institutional path and its resulting economic development. The authors confront the observation, wrestled with by many institutional and development scholars, that some countries have institutions and practices that resist change even when those institutions hold back economic progress and when change would be desirable. Under such circumstances, governments and international organizations often introduce policies meant to jolt or shock people out of their previous ways of living (2008: 332). However, forced institutional change can fail, the authors contend, whenever the externally imposed institutions fail to reflect the "metis" of the group meant to be impacted. As they explain,

> A concept passed down from the ancient Greeks, metis is characterized by local knowledge resulting from practical experience. It includes skills, culture, norms, and conventions, which are shaped by the experiences of the individual. This concept applies to both interactions between people (e.g., interpreting the gestures and actions of others) and the physical environment (e.g., learning to ride a bike). The components of metis cannot be written down neatly as a systematic set of instructions. Instead, knowledge regarding metis is gained only through experience and practice. (2008: 338)

We can see how a group's metis relates to its social stock of knowledge and its culture. Metis describes a particular set of ways of seeing and interpreting the world that have been learned over time and through shared experiences. Because institutions have a higher likelihood of adoption when they align with a group's metis, metis can also be thought of as "the glue that gives institutions their stickiness" (2008: 338). To demonstrate how metis can affect the success of institutional change, the authors contrast Poland and Russia after their transition from communism to a market economy. Since Polish people historically engaged in private businesses, they had already developed a metis conducive to the newly introduced formal institutions of privatization. Russia, however, lacked this metis. Therefore, while Poland's economy developed more smoothly in the years following its transition, the privatized Russian economy was beset with corruption and theft of state property.

Grube's (2015) work on the politics of communal land tenure in South Africa, for instance, illustrates the uniqueness of the Austrian conception of culture. Grube focused attention on the Gumbi community of KwaZulu Natal, South Africa, seeking to explain the persistence of traditional institutions of land governance there in the face of attempts by municipal governments to replace traditional governance structures with formal governance structures. In the Gumbi community, land is communally owned and cannot be titled or sold. Chiefs, with the help of their advisory councils, preside over several matters, including those related to land allocation. While poverty is high and businesses do not easily form, in part relating to the lack of private property rights, the Gumbi hold on to their traditional system governance of land. Grube conducted thirteen interviews in 2007 and 2009 in order to interrogate this conundrum. The use of qualitative techniques enabled the author to sort between standard economic explanations and cultural explanations for the persistence of traditional land governance institutions. Grube found explanations pointing to rent-seeking on the part of traditional leaders as well as a lack of competition wanting, and posited instead that "[c]ultural beliefs that underlie traditional leadership help the institution 'stick'" (2015: 377).

Grube argues that the persistence of traditional leadership can be explained with reference to the Gumbi's cultural system, which synchronizes the Gumbi's ethos with their worldview. In particular, the Gumbi revere their current traditional leaders because their unique identity is bound up with them having traditional leaders, going back generations to the group's first leader, Shaka. If the Gumbi's identity was not in part based on having traditional leaders, the Gumbi might not experience any loss of identity in moving toward a different system of governance over land matters. However, because community members value their unique identity, they value the chief's input in community decisions, especially in matters related to communal property, where chiefs are viewed as "custodians" of communal land (2015: 381). Furthermore, the Gumbi see themselves as having a strong relationship with their ancestors, who they believe are always are watching over them from the land. The Gumbi believe that "ancestors reside on family plots in communal plots and that communications with ancestors can only take place from the grave site" (2015: 381). Community members therefore value the ability to conduct important ceremonies like weddings or funerals on the land, so their ancestors can take part in these. To forfeit land to municipal government could therefore break the link that the Gumbi have to their ancestors, leaving them feeling direction-less. Lastly, Grube argued that the Gumbi were suspicious of freehold titles and alternative forms of property ownership thanks to "a long history of intervention and land confiscation" under apartheid and before (2015: 390). As a result of this worldview, the Gumbi favored retaining traditional leadership over communal property, as to them this meant that they were secure from injustice.

In a similar way, Chamlee-Wright (1997) operationalized the Geertzian conception of culture in order to shed light on entrepreneurship among women in urban Ghana. Similar to Grube (2015), Chamlee-Wright considered why formal interventions into Ghanaian markets by the Ghanaian government and international organizations, who tried to stimulate indigenous entrepreneurship, for example, through various credit schemes, were not always successful. Chamlee-Wright points out that by paying close attention to indigenous markets, we can see how cultural contexts dictate rules governing credit acquisition, capital accumulation, and other corporate practices. For Chamlee-Wright (1997: 24), "[n]ot only does culture provide the 'glue' which enables social institutions to stick, it is the context in which individuals make sense of the world around them." While it is important and useful to think of culture as that which explains why some institutions 'stick' and others don't, the unique contribution of Austrian economics to cultural understanding is to illuminate how culture affects the meanings people find in their worlds, meanings which, in turn, influence how people build and navigate their economic lives.

Pinpointing the cultural foundations of urban female entrepreneurship in Ghana, Chamlee-Wright argues that the Akan of Ghana believe that God gives everyone a unique personal destiny – a "nkrabea" – that guides their activities, including their entrepreneurial activities. Chamlee-Wright claims that this concept is the basis of a work ethic in Ghana. The Akan also practice an ethic of supporting their kin, hence market traders often view their economic success in markets as a means to help out family, in business with capital, or at home with services like childcare. They further believe that their ancestral spirits guide them and consider elders to be stewards. This belief partly explains why older women ("market queens") receive more respect in the market and can dictate the activities of younger ones.

Chamlee-Wright described how, in spite of particular constraints facing Ghanaian women, including discrimination and lack of resources, they are still highly engaged in entrepreneurship. As Chamlee-Wright (1997: 112–113) states,

> Though men are privileged over women in both the matrilineal and patrilineal inheritance structures, women are adapting in ways that will concentrate accumulated capital within the hands of the entrepreneurs they train – their daughters, grand-daughters, and nieces. As women acquire more individual property, they are employing the use of written wills more frequently to override traditional inheritance structures.

This entrepreneurial focus among Ghanaian women, Chamlee-Wright explains, occurs because of their obligation to their children, and because indigenous trade was a long-established tradition in Ghana, with many institutions evolving to support it.

In the same vein, Chamlee-Wright (2002) addresses those scholars who believe that Zimbabwean culture is resistant to entrepreneurship and a capitalist ethic. After conducting 150 interviews in Zimbabwe between January and June 1999, she was able to describe the strategies that urban market women use in order to save and invest, despite the severe constraints that they face. As she describes (2002: 1002),

> Zimbabwean history, culture, and political economy often appear to be pitted against female entrepreneurs; nonetheless, traders have cultivated strategies for responding to this context in ways that promote hard work, thrift, the maintenance and growth of capital, and a creative search for profitable business ventures and investments ... strategies such as participating in rotating credit and mutual assistance organizations, hoarding nonperishable stocks, converting cash into assets that will hold their value, engaging in multiple business activities, and finding ways to maintain control over resources are more than just mere survival strategies. Such strategies are potentially the seeds of a growing capitalist ethic and entrepreneurial class.

Chamlee-Wright's work therefore serves as a model for how economists can use qualitative approaches to study particular markets, and to understand how culture infuses people with particular meanings that affect their economic decision-making.

An additional benefit of this approach is that it avoids treating cultures as static. Indeed, Chamlee-Wright finds that the Zimbabwean market women saving and investment strategies evolved to fit their cultural background. Note also that Chamlee-Wright is simply trying to understand how the women approach and navigate their economic lives by interpreting their constraints. As such, she is not comparing Zimbabwean culture with any other in order to argue for its social or economic progressiveness or backwardness. As she maintains (2002: 1001), "No culture is completely supportive or completely resistant to women's economic activities."

Further, Chamlee-Wright and Storr (2010b, 2011) led interviews with 301 subjects in various parts of New Orleans to examine people's actions in the aftermath of Hurricane Katrina, in particular, to see up close how communities come together to resolve the complex social coordination problems that emerge in the aftermath of natural disasters. Interviews were conducted three years after the storm, and the authors supplemented interview data with newspaper and other media accounts. Interview subjects included residents, business owners and managers, church pastors, nonprofit directors and employees, and rental property owners. The interview team asked open-ended questions in order get at the kinds of help and services that were provided to residents by members of the community, and to examine the various motivations and challenges surrounding the community redevelopment efforts of social entrepreneurs.

Specifically, Chamlee-Wright and Storr (2011) sort to uncover the meaning behind people's actions in St. Bernard Parish, a community just outside of Orleans Parish, after Hurricane Katrina. The goal was to understand what was signified by the people's community rebuilding efforts in the aftermath of Hurricane Katrina. Chamlee-Wright and Storr found that, for members of St. Bernard Parish, activities surrounding work held a particular meaning for members of the community. Chamlee-Wright and Storr (2011: 278) observed that "physical work, such as the work associated with mucking out and repairing homes badly damaged by flood and toxic contamination, was not viewed as something to be feared or looked down upon," but instead these activities signified "a challenge worthy of the experience and fortitude commonly found within the community." Thus, in addition to the family-oriented values of the community and their celebration of their community's history, the people of St. Bernard Parish promulgated narratives of hard work and self-reliance, which thus oriented them through their rebuilding efforts.

Beyond St. Bernard Parish, members of the Vietnamese community of New Orleans and early returnees to the Ninth Ward also built their recovery strategies around collective narratives (Chamlee-Wright and Storr 2011). For the retur-nees, the Mary Queen of Vietnam Catholic Church community symbolized a "second homeland." According to the authors, this collective narrative about the community "arguably made returning and rebuilding rather than resetting elsewhere the preferred option" (2011: 271). The authors pointed that what was getting said by the returning and rebuilding actions of the Vietnamese commu-nity was a confidence in their plans to rebuild their community, a belief that their success in this regard was divinely intended, and a particular satisfaction with their way of life in community, inspiring a desire to return to the way things once were.

Chamlee-Wright and Storr (2010a) focused on social entrepreneurship as being critical to the post-disaster recovery process. As they wrote,

> Social entrepreneurs perform important social functions before, during and after a disaster. Before a disaster they are an important source of information to residents in their communities about the impending danger and how to prepare for it. They also organise evacuations, ensuring that community members leave vulnerable areas and are able to make it to nearby shelters. In the immediate aftermath of a disaster, social entrepre-neurs organise community members to search for their missing neigh-bours, to advocate for government resources and the restoration of public

services and to pool their resources to feed, shelter and otherwise care for their neighbours who have suffered during the disaster. In the months and years following a disaster, they help to coordinate recovery efforts, lobby for essential government assistance and provide key information and services to help displaced residents return and rebuild their communities. (Chamlee-Wright and Storr 2010a: 153)

Chamlee-Wright and Storr demonstrate using a qualitative approach how shared meanings motivate particular patterns of action within communities, in a way that would not be possible using a quantitative approach. For example, they were able to focus in on the actions of Doris Voitier, superintendent of the St. Bernard Parish Unified School District, a social entrepreneur who was key in "[r]ecognizing the importance of a functioning school system to long term community recovery – both as a key feature of any vibrant community and an important signal to displaced residents that the community would, indeed, come back" (2010a: 156). Voitier created portable classrooms and committed to reopen the schools by a particular date. Her actions were interpreted by the community as a positive sign of community redevelopment, and signified hope for them, which encouraged them to return. Similarly, Father Vien, the pastor of the Mary Queen of Vietnam Catholic Church, was another social entrepreneur who, interviews showed, was crucial in bringing people to the New Orleans East Vietnamese community. Father Vien visited evacuation sites, checked on his parishioners, resumed services just six weeks after the hurricane, and used his services to urge displaced congregants to move back to the community. According to Chamlee-Wright and Storr, Father Vien's actions had at least two meanings: they "sent a powerful signal to those who had not yet returned that the community would indeed rebound; thereby mitigating the collective action problem that typically faces evacuees," and his "well-attended services also sent a powerful signal to government officials, making it clear that the members of this community intended to return and rebuild" (2010a: 156). The qualitative approach enabled Chamlee-Wright and Storr to understand how culture shaped the redevelopment successes in the New Orleans context.

Storr explicitly invokes Weber's use of economic spirits and finds that competing economic spirits shaped Bahamian capitalism in the twentieth century (Storr 2004, 2013). Storr characterized the particular form of capitalism existing in the Bahamas at that time with reference to the following facts – relatively strong macroeconomic performance, high levels of self-employment and entrepreneurial creativity, especially in the tourism and Junkanoo industries, a cycle of booms and busts, low capital intensity, poor customer service, and high levels of rent-seeking and corruption.

For Storr, Bahamians were animated in their dealings by two competing spirits – the "spirit of Rabbyism" and the "spirit of Junkanoo." The former celebrated piracy, guile, and getting something for nothing. Economic actors animated by this spirit might be businesspeople trying to trick their consumers into paying for a defective product, or politicians accepting bribes in exchange for special protections for certain companies. Linguistic expression of this piratical spirit could be found in Bahamian folktales, which prominently featured a character who embodied all of these features: B'Rabby. According to Storr (2013: 74), Bahamian folklore celebrates B'Rabby, who "while rejecting greediness, nonetheless believes that he is entitled to whatever he can steal (and get away with), that it is alright to have a casual relationship with the truth, and that cunning is a necessary tool for survival." On the other hand, the spirit of Junkanoo vies with the spirit of Rabbyism to influence economic life in the Bahamas.

While Rabbyism steers Bahamians toward cheating and corruption in their dealings, the spirit of Junkanoo infuses Bahamians with a respect for hard work and long-term planning, creativity and flair, and collaboration and unity. Junkanoo is a semiannual cultural festival that takes place in the Bahamas, and is at the heart of the cultural identity of Bahamians of all ethnic backgrounds. Bahamians spend the year preparing for the festival together – designing and fabricating costumes, creating music and choreography, and organizing parades and competitions. The spirit of Junkanoo flows through Bahamians as they prepare for Junkanoo, work to send their children to school, or provide services to tourists. According to Storr, all Bahamians contend with a "spirit of Rabbyism," which encourages them to use trickery to get ahead, and a "spirit of Junkanoo," which encourages them to succeed by working hard, planning, and being creative. Again, one of the many advantages of examining the capitalist spirits that animate markets using qualitative strategies is that economists avoid treating cultures as homogenous. In Storr's investigation, the spirit of Rabbyism in the Bahamas is offset by the Junkanoo ethic. Arguably, it is impossible to notice these dualities within a society using methods that involve aggregate statistics.

Utilizing Bahamian history to explore the origins of these particular spirits, Storr (2004) shows that during the seventeenth and eighteenth centuries, pirates in the West Indies chiefly operated out of the Bahamas. In subsequent epochs, ships were wrecked and ransacked for their booty, and contraband guns, rum, and drugs were smuggled to the USA. Through experience with these enterprises, Bahamians learned that quick and great wealth could come from engaging in illegal activity. In addition, slavery and colonization oppressed black Bahamians, who in response embraced tales of mythical heroes who could outsmart their oppressors. Storr also argues that Bahamians' enterprising spirit could also be traced back to slavery. The Bahamas did not develop a plantation economy system like other Caribbean colonies, as Bahamian soil was not conducive to the large-scale production of sugar or cotton. Since the opportunity cost of permitting slaves certain freedoms was low, Bahamian planters often gave slaves "use rights" over portions of plantations, the freedom to sell whatever crops they could grow in markets, and even the freedom to sell their own labor in exchange for cash fees paid to planters. Bahamian slaves took advantage of these opportunities to develop themselves economically, and learned to tie work and personal economic success together.

Additionally, Storr and John (2013) use interviews to investigate differences in self-employment rates among the major ethnic groups represented in Trinidad and Tobago. Storr and John (2013) examine census figures in Trinidad and Tobago to demonstrate patterns of entrepreneurial exploitation (proxied by reported self-employment figures) in Trinidad and Tobago. They find, even after controlling for individual characteristics that could impact a person's decision to become self-employed, that African or black Trinidadians have the lowest rates of self-employment, Indians and mixed Trinidadians have the second highest rates, and that Chinese, Syrian-Lebanese, and white Trinidadians have the highest probability of being self-employed of all ethnic groups. To explain these differences, they argue that people in Trinidad and Tobago assess the opportunity to become entrepreneurs through a variety of cultural lenses. While Trinidadians tend to identify specific opportunities for entrepreneurial gain due to, for example, membership in ethnically based social networks that encourage opportunity identification, one of the deleterious effects of slavery and colonization was that people learned to prioritize work in the public sector and academic pursuits, at the expense of business pursuits. Storr and John use the interview data to substantiate the various historical/sociological factors that they hypothesize might explain differences in ethnic self-employment rates in Trinidad and Tobago. As such, they demonstrate that qualitative approaches can be used to tell complex stories about the relationship between culture and entrepreneurship.

John and Storr (2018) also conducted interviews with twenty-five members of the labor force (eleven regular employees, six managers, six business owners, an economist/public official, and a journalist), the results of which established a pattern of entrepreneurial identification among Trinidadians in general. As

John and Storr (2018) explain, scholars of entrepreneurship sometimes divide the entrepreneurial process into two stages. In the first stage, a person identifies or sees an entrepreneurial opportunity. A belief in the primacy of the first stage can be attributed to Austrian economist Israel Kirzner. For Kirzner, what distinguishes the entrepreneur is the fact that they see an opportunity to make money, an opportunity that exists because some earlier entrepreneur failed to notice it, or made a mistake, for example by setting too high or too low a price, by hiring the wrong workers, or by failing to offer a product or service for which there is clear demand. On the other hand, for Joseph Schumpeter, another Austrian economist, the essence of entrepreneurship was in the second stage – the exploitation of the entrepreneurial opportunity. Seeing an opportunity was not enough for something to be entrepreneurship. For Schumpeter, anyone could dream up a new way of doing things in their mind. Only the activity of the leader or entrepreneur who carries out the idea is what actually matters for technical progress.

A total of 60 percent of their interview subjects had expressed explicit plans to open businesses and described those plans in some detail. Explicit areas of business indicated by subjects included "interior design, buying and selling Haitian art, customized baking, architecture, transportation of school children, comfort shoes, and cosmetology" (John and Storr 2018). Interviews also revealed subjects' personal reasons for not having acted on their business plans yet.

Trinidad and Tobago, a high-income Caribbean country whose main exports include oil and gas, has been analyzed in the Austrian tradition of studying culture, that is, examined for its competing economic spirits, models, and metaphors. Recall, Storr and John (2013) demonstrated that economic life in Trinidad and Tobago could be characterized by low or uneven exploitation of entrepreneurial opportunities among social groups, while at the same time Trinidadians in general were quite in the habit of identifying entrepreneurial opportunities (John and Storr 2018). This important feature of Trinidadian capitalism – low and uneven opportunity exploitation relative to opportunity identification – could partially be explained with reference to competing economic spirits at work in Trinidad and Tobago, spirits that might be referred to as a "cavalier spirit" and a "courtier spirit." Both spirits find their origin in the unique history, culture, institutions, and resource endowments of Trinidad and Tobago.

The cavalier spirit animates Trinidadians in markets, making them alert to profit opportunities, eager to make rich and detailed business plans, and willing to exploit them. The Trinidadian cavalier is also seeking personal gain through involvement in the business enterprise. However, the cavalier does not consider the government as a crux. Indeed, in some instances in Trinidad and Tobago, the cavalier entrepreneur is flouting laws and legal standards of business practice in order to attain their goals. Cavaliers approach business in an audacious, sometimes reckless way. These entrepreneurs often grasp at opportunities that other entrepreneurs do not consider to be dignified sources of profit.

On the other hand, the courtier spirit privileges political connections and appointments, and believes that responsibility for industry and work should be in the hands of political actors. The courtier spirit represents the tendency of some Trinidadian entrepreneurs to seek favors from the state in order to gain a competitive advantage in business or in life in general. As such, the typical courtier tends to support and be dependent on the government in a manner that one may describe as being parasitic. What the government provides for the Trinidadian courtier is mainly privileged information and access to opportunities for personal gain. Courtiers also prefer to engage in traditional business activities that guarantee steady profits. They are typically unwilling to experiment outside of established industries. Although an opportunistic attitude toward the state may describe businesspeople in almost any context, particularly where governments are corrupt or heavily intervene in the economy, the specific courtier spirit that we suggest now exists in Trinidad and Tobago can be traced back to unique events in the history of the country.

John and Storr (2018) argue that there are several reasons for the competing entrepreneurial orientations of Trinidadians, that of the cavalier and that of the courtesan. During colonization, Britain transplanted its institutions of private property, rule of law, and freedom of contract in Trinidad and Tobago. Over time, Trinidadians learned to recognize and embrace the particular economic freedoms that facilitated entrepreneurship. In addition, John and Storr (2018: 595) argued that independence in 1962 encouraged a discourse in Trinidad and Tobago that reflected "people's desire to build up the country and turn it into something distinctly Trinidadian." On the other hand, the adoption of a British-style welfare state after 1962 taught Trinidadians a different set of lessons. The authors argue that "the political culture teaches Trinidadians that they are unable to succeed without assistance and that they are owed favors from the government," and also that "that the government will capture the fruits of entrepreneurial discoveries" (2018: 595). Finally, the authors showed how ethnically based social networks could facilitate entrepreneurial opportunity identification while hampering opportunity exploitation among the various ethnic groups in Trinidad and Tobago.

In sum, both spirits of enterprise – courtier and cavalier – serve as general metaphors to describe Trinidad and Tobago's contemporary business culture. Furthermore, while both spirits of enterprise seem to contradict each other, it is possible and even likely that, as Storr (2004, 2013) pointed, any Trinidadian entrepreneur may demonstrate both the courtier and cavalier spirit of enterprise in their approach to business.

6 Conclusion

Austrian economics offers a unique approach to the study of culture in economic life. For Austrian economists, culture must not be excluded from economic analysis, but taken seriously and brought to the fore. Austrian economists take culture, like Geertz and like Weber, to be the webs of significance in which "man is suspended" and "which he himself has spun" (Geertz 1973: 8). Austrian economics sees culture as patterns of meanings, as a lens through which people view the world, as opposed to collections of beliefs of values, or a tool of economic success. Finally, Austrian economics proceeds with cultural analysis by seeking to uncover any and all economic spirits, models, and metaphors that animate people's economic lives in various contexts.

Of course, not all self-identified Austrian economists consistently adopt this approach.[16] For instance, adopting a non-Austrian approach, Williamson and Coyne (2013) utilize the Economic Freedom of the World Index to measure countries' institutions of economic freedom, and the World Values Survey to measure countries' culture. Searching for a relationship between the two, they find that "cultures with high levels of trust, respect, self-control, and lacking obedience help to facilitate free trade and access to sound money" (2013: 94).

Similarly, Harper (2003) reasons that cultures where people function as though they exert control over their own lives will embrace entrepreneurship to a greater extent than cultures where people believe external forces dictate their destinies. To this effect, Harper references empirical work by Chia et al. (1998) that shows that US college students exhibit a stronger internal locus of control relative to their Taiwanese counterparts, in order to suggest that Americans potentially could be more likely to actively start businesses rather

---

[16] As the examples here show, economists who self-identify as Austrian economists do not uniformly ascribe to the approach that sees culture as a framework of meaning, nor do they all embrace qualitative analyses of culture. We contend, however, that the approach to studying culture that is most consistent with the Austrian tradition of economics is the Geertzian approach, as articulated by Lavoie. As demonstrated earlier in Section 2, Geertz built on Weber to understand culture as meaning, and the links between Geertz and Weber's economic sociology are as well-established as Weber's links to Austrian economics.

than to passively seek employment, as a result of a difference in culture (Harper 2003).

Runst (2013) showed how culture and institutions are deeply intertwined, and how lessons learned under a particular set of political institutions at one point in history can influence how people approach markets even once those institutions change. Runst examined Germany's political and economic history in conjunction with the development of a cultural lens that placed a particular gaze on market and state activity. Before Germany was reunified under a single legal and political framework in 1989, East Germans lived for over forty years under totalitarian and socialist institutions. Runst considered whether Germans in the eastern part of the country would, after 1989, embrace markets by starting private business at the same rate as those in the Western part. Runst found that between 1996 and 2004, Eastern Germany had roughly 27 percent fewer start-ups than Western Germany (2013: 614). Runst attributed part of this difference to culture, arguing that "the unique socialist history in East Germany exerted a persistent but declining influence on the beliefs and preferences of its inhabitants and temporarily reduced rates of self-employment" (2013: 619).

Runst suggested that East Germans had adapted to their repressive political and economic institutions, such that "minds that developed during a prolonged period of socialism" (2013: 595) experienced an "inner struggle" (2013: 600) when it came to seizing the business opportunities that reunification made legal. Although Germans raised in the East may have had the same tendency to notice entrepreneurial opportunities as Germans from the West, the former may have been more inclined to not follow through on those opportunities, especially in the years right after reunification. Runst argued that their initial hesitance toward starting businesses reflected a "command culture" that developed in East Germany. East Germans had grown accustomed to lacking control over their own lives and to "being tossed around by forces beyond one's reach" (2013: 598). They had been under constant watch by government and citizens, and therefore had grown accustomed to conformity. Finally, East Germans had developed a sense that markets were "chaotic and unjust" (2013: 604), since, under socialism, those who profited were those with suspicious political ties. Using survey data from the German Socio-Economic Panel, Runst predicted that persons from the eastern part of Germany were more likely to prefer state intervention over private entrepreneurship to address social problems and vulnerability, and were more likely to believe luck and fate directed people's lives as opposed to their own deliberate control. In considering the history of East and West Germans, therefore, Runst shows Germany as not culturally homogenous, but diverse and evolving – over time as well as space.

Admittedly, approaching the study of culture in economic life using the Austrian method is not without its difficulties. For one, efforts to understand how people actually experience markets using fieldwork are bound to be financially burdensome and generally more taxing on researchers. Conducting interviews, archival work, and case studies often require significant outlays of money and time and patience, due to travel expenses, the difficulties of cross-cultural communication, and the complexities of navigating a different culture in which the expectations of the researchers and their subjects may clash. The more pernicious biases of researchers/subjects may also prevent fruitful exchange and interpretation from taking place. Furthermore, the "objectivist" bias examined by Lavoie (1991) ultimately may make it difficult for cultural researchers in the economic mainstream to get published in high-ranked economic journals or to gain access to lucrative appointments by using qualitative techniques in their work on culture.

For those who find a way to embrace this method, however, promising research awaits. While a path exists for doing culturally aware research on the economic spirits influencing entrepreneurship and other traditionally "economic" activities, interesting qualitative scholarship might also pay attention to the cultural context of actors embedded in political and legal institutions. Furthermore, Lavoie's focus on uncovering the interpretive and linguistic schemes of markets should also inspire examinations of the social nature of markets, as opposed to solely thinking of markets as "economic" processes. Storr (2013: 98–99) describes how, contrary to the opinions of some, the market is not a cold, impersonal space, but rather a deeply meaningful space (like the home or the church), where people's lives play out, where people build relationships, and where people develop their character, identities, and aspirations. As such, future cultural work in the Austrian tradition should examine the immense range of social processes that emerge under various institutional settings and against a diversity of cultural backdrops.

References

Aghion, P., Algan, Y., Cahuc, P., & Shleifer, A. (2010) "Regulation and Distrust," *The Quarterly Journal of Economics*, 125(3): 1015–1049.

Alesina, A., Algan, Y., Cahuc, P., & Giuliano, P. (2015). "Family Values and the Regulation of Labor," *Journal of the European Economic Association*, 13(4): 599–630.

Alesina, A., & Giuliano, P. (2015). "Culture and Institutions," *Journal of Economic Literature*, 53(4): 898–944.

Algan, Y., & Cahuc, P. (2009). "Civic Virtue and Labor Market Institutions," *American Economic Journal: Macroeconomics*, 1(1): 111–145.

Algan, Y., & Cahuc, P. (2010). "Inherited Trust and Growth," *American Economic Review*, 100(5): 2060–2092.

Allison, J., & Lin, L. (1999). "The Evolution of Chinese Attitudes toward Property Rights in Invention and Discovery," *University of Pennsylvania Journal of International Economic Law*, 20(4): 735–791.

Aoki, M., Kuran, T., & Roland, G. (2012). *Institutions and Comparative Economic Development*, Basingstoke: Palgrave Macmillan.

Bertrand, M., Erzo, F., Luttmer, P., & Mullainathan, S. (2000). "Network Effects and Welfare Cultures," *The Quarterly Journal of Economics*, 115(3): 1019–1055.

Bertrand, M., & Schoar, A. (2006). "The Role of Family in Family Firms," *The Journal of Economic Perspectives*, 20(2): 73–96.

Boettke, P. (1998a). "Why Culture Matters: Economics, Politics and the Imprint of History," Ama-gi: The Journal of the Hayek Society at the London School of Economics, 2(1): 9–16.

Boettke, P. (1998b). "Rational Choice and Human Agency in Economics and Sociology: Exploring the Weber-Austrian Connection." In H. Giersch (ed.), *Merits and Limits of Markets*, Berlin: Springer: 53–81.

Boettke, P., Coyne, C., & Leeson, P. (2008). "Institutional Stickiness and the New Development Economics," *American Journal of Economics and Sociology*, 67(2): 331–358.

Boettke, P., & Storr, V. (2002). "Post Classical Political Economy," *American Journal of Economics and Sociology*, 61(1):161–191.

Bourdieu, P. (1977).*Outline of a Theory of Practice*, Cambridge: Cambridge University Press.

Buchan, N., Croson, R., & Johnson, E. (2004). "When Do Fair Beliefs Influence Bargaining Behavior? Experimental Bargaining in Japan and the United States," *Journal of Consumer Research*, 31(1): 18–190.

Burlando, R., & Hey, J. D. (1997)."Do Anglo-Saxons Free-ride More?" *Journal of Public Economics*, 64(1): 41–60.

Carpenter, J., Daniere, A., & Takahasi, L. (2004) "Cooperation, Trust, and Social Capital in Southeast Asian Urban Slums," *Journal of Economic Behavior and Organization*, 55: 533–551.

Chamlee-Wright, E. (1997). *The Cultural Foundations of Economic Development: Urban Female Entrepreneurship in Ghana*, New York: Routledge.

Chamlee-Wright, E. (2002). "Savings and Accumulation Strategies of Urban Market Women in Harare, Zimbabwe," *Economic Development and Cultural Change*, 50(4): 979–1005.

Chamlee-Wright, E. (2010). *The Cultural and Political Economy of Recovery: Social Learning in a Post-Disaster Environment*, New York: Routledge.

Chamlee-Wright, E. (2011). "Operationalizing the Interpretive Turn: Deploying Qualitative Methods Toward an Economics of Meaning," *Review of Austrian Economics*, 24: 158–170.

Chamlee-Wright, E., & Storr, V. (2010a). "The Role of Social Entrepreneurship in Post-Katrina Community Recovery." In E. Chamlee-Wright & V. Storr (eds.), *The Political Economy of Hurricane Katrina and Community Rebound*, Cheltenham: Edward Elgar: 87–106.

Chamlee-Wright, E., & Storr, V. (2010b). "Community Resilience in New Orleans East: Deploying the Cultural Toolkit within a Vietnamese-American Community." In J. Rivera and D. Miller (eds.), *Community Disaster Recovery and Resiliency: Exploring Global Opportunities and Challenges*, New York: CRC Press: 101–124.

Chamlee-Wright, E., & Storr, V. (2011). "Social Capital as Collective Narratives and Post-Disaster Community Recovery," *Sociological Review*, 59(2): 266–282.

Chia, R., Cheng, B., & Chuang, C. (1998). "Differentiation in the Source of Internal Control for Chinese," *Journal of Social Behavior & Personality*, 13(4): 565–578.

Chow, G. (2010). *Interpreting China's Economy*, Hackensack, NJ: World Scientific Publishing.

Chuah, S.-H., Hoffman, R., Jones, M., & Williams, G. (2007). "Do Cultures Clash? Evidence from Cross-national Ultimatum Game Experiments," *Journal of Economic Behavior and Organization*, 64 (1): 35–48.

Fan, C.-P. (2000). "Teaching Children Cooperation – An Application of Experimental Game Theory," *Journal of Economic Behavior and Organization*, 41(3): 191–209.

Fehr, E., & Leibbrandt, A. (2011). "A Field study on Cooperativeness and Impatience in the Tragedy of the Commons," *Journal of Public Economics*, 95(9): 1144–1155.

Fernández, R., & Fogli, A. (2009). "Culture: An Empirical Investigation of Beliefs, Work, and Fertility," *American Economic Journal: Macroeconomics*, 1(1): 146–177.

Fisman, R., & Miguel, E. (2007). "Corruption, Norms and Legal Enforcement: Evidence from Diplomatic Parking Tickets," *Journal of Political Economy*, 115(6): 1020–1048.

Gadamer, H. (1976). *Philosophical Hermeneutics*. Berkeley, CA: University of California Press.

Geertz, C. (1973). *The Interpretation of Cultures*, New York: Basic Books.

Gorodnichenko, Y., & Roland, G. (2011). "Which Dimensions of Culture Matter for Long Run Growth?" *American Economic Review*, 101(3): 492–498.

Gorodnichenko, Y., & Roland, G. (2017). "Culture, Institutions, and the Wealth of Nations," *Review of Economics and Statistics*, 99(3): 402–416.

Greif, A. (1994) "Cultural Beliefs and the Organization of Society: A Historical and Theoretical Reflection on Collectivist and Individualist Societies," *Journal of Political Economy*, 102(5): 912–950.

Grube, L. (2015). "The Role of Culture in the Persistence of Traditional Leadership: Evidence from KwaZulu Natal, South Africa." In L. Grube & V. Storr (eds.), *Culture and Economic Action*, Northampton: Edward Elgar: 375–397.

Gudeman, S. (1986). *Economics as Culture: Models and Metaphors of Livelihood*, London: Routledge.

Guiso, L., Sapienza P., & Zingales, L. (2004). "The Role of Social Capital in Financial Development," *The American Economic Review*, 94(3): 526–556.

Guiso, L., Sapienaza P., & Zingales, L. (2006). "Does Culture Affect Economic Outcomes?" *Journal of Economic Perspectives*, 20(2): 23–48.

Guiso, L., Sapienza P., & Zingales, L. (2009). "Cultural Biases in Economic Exchange?" *Quarterly Journal of Economics*, 124(3): 1095–1131.

Harper, D. (2003). *Foundations of Entrepreneurship and Economic Development*, New York: Routledge.

Harrison, L. (1992) *Who Prospers: How Cultural Values Shape Economic and Political Success*, New York: BasicBooks.

Harrison, L. (2008). *The Central Liberal Truth: How Politics Can Change a Culture and Save It from Itself*, New York: Oxford University Press.

Harrison, L., & Huntington, S. (2000). *Culture Matters: How Values Shape Human Progress*, New York: BasicBooks.

Hayek, F. (1948). *Individualism and Economic Order*, Chicago: University of Chicago Press.

Hayek, F. (1952). *The Counter Revolution of Science: Studies on the Abuse of Reason*, Glencoe, IL: The Free Press.

Hayek, F. (1973). *Law, Legislation and Liberty Volume 1: Rules and Order*, Chicago: University of Chicago Press.

Hayek, F. A. (1952). *The Sensory Order*, Chicago: University of Chicago Press.

Hemesath, M., & Pomponio, X. (1998). "Cooperation and Culture: Students from China and the United States in a Prisoner's Dilemma," *Cross-Cultural Research: The Journal of Comparative Social Science*, 32(2): 171–184.

Henrich, J. (2000). "Does Culture Matter in Economic Behavior? Ultimatum Game Bargaining among the Machiguenga of the Peruvian Amazon," *The American Economic Review*, 90(4): 973–979.

Henrich, J., Boyd, R., Bowles, S., et al. (2001). "In Search of Homo Economicus: Behavioral Experiments in 15 Small-Scale Societies," *The American Economic Review*, 91(2): 73–78.

Hofstede, G. (2001). *Culture's Consequences: Comparing Values, Behaviors, Institutions and Organizations across Nations*, Thousand Oaks, CA: Sage Publications.

Holm, H. J., & Danielson, A. (2005). "Tropic Trust versus Nordic Trust: Experimental Evidence from Tanzania And Sweden," *The Economic Journal*, 115: 505–532.

John, A., & Storr, V. (2018). "Kirznerian and Schumpeterian Entrepreneurship in Trinidad and Tobago," *Journal of Enterprising Communities: People and Places in the Global Economy*, 12(5): 582–610.

Knack, S. (2001). "Trust, Associational Life and Economic Performance." In J. F. Helliwell (ed.), *The Contribution of Human and Social Capital to Sustained Economic Growth and Well-Being*, Quebec: Human Resources Development Canada: 172–202.

Knack, S., & Keefer, P. (1997). "Does Social Capital Have an Economic Payoff? A Cross-Country Investigation," *The Quarterly Journal of Economics*, 112(4): 1251–1288.

Knack, S., & Zak, P. (2001). "Trust and Growth," *The Economic Journal*, 111 (470): 295–321.

Knight, F. (1925). "Fact and Metaphysics in Economic Psychology," *The American Economic Review*, 15(2): 247–266.

La Porta, R., Lopez-de-Silanes, F., Shleifer, A., & Vishny, R. W. (1997). "Trust in Large Organizations," *The American Economic Review*, 87(2): 333–338.

Lavoie, D. (1991). "The Discovery and Interpretation of Profit Opportunities: Culture and the Kirznerian Entrepreneur." In B. Berger (ed.), *The Culture of Entrepreneurship*, San Francisco: ICS Press: 33–51.

Lavoie, D. (2011). "The Interpretive Dimension of Economics: Science, Hermeneutics, and Praxeology," *Review of Austrian Economics*, 24: 91–128.

Lavoie, D., & Chamlee-Wright, E. (2000) *Culture and Enterprise: The Development, Representation, and Morality of Business*, New York: Routledge.

Levy, Jr., M. (1962). "Some Aspects of 'Individualism' and the Problem of Modernization in China and Japan," *Economic Development and Cultural Change*, 10(3): 225–240.

Mathers, R., & Williamson, C. (2011). "Cultural Context: Explaining the Productivity of Capitalism," *Kyklos*, 64(2): 231–252.

Menger, C. (1892). "On the Origins of Money," *History of Economic Thought Articles*, 2: 239–255.

Mises, L. (1949). *Human Action: A Treatise on Economics*, San Francisco: Fox & Wilkes.

Mises, L. (1957). *Theory and History: An Interpretation of Social and Economic Evolution*, New Haven, CT: Yale University Press.

Mokyr, J. (2017). *A Culture of Growth: The Origins of the Modern Economy*, Princeton, NJ; Oxford: Princeton University Press.

Ockenfels, A., & Weimann, J. (1999). "Types and Patterns: An Experimental East-West-German Comparison of Cooperation and Solidarity," *Journal of Public Economics*, 71(2): 275–287.

Pye, L. (2000). "'Asian Values': From Dynamos to Dominoes?" In L. Harrison & S. Huntington (eds.), *Culture Matters: How Values Shape Human Progress*, New York: Basic Books, 244–255.

Roth, A., Prasnikar, V., Okuno-Fujiwara, M., & Zamir, S. (1991) "Bargaining and Market Behavior in Jerusalem, Ljubljana, Pittsburgh, and Tokyo: An Experimental Study,"*The American Economic Review*, 81 (5): 1068–1095.

Runst, P. (2013). "Post-Socialist Culture and Entrepreneurship," *American Journal of Economics and Sociology*, 72(3): 593–626.

Ryle, G. (2009) [1968]. "The Thinking of Thoughts: What Is 'Le Penseur' Doing?" In *Collected Essays 1929–1968: Collected Papers, Volume 2*, London: Routledge, 494–510.

Schütz, A. (1967). *The Phenomenology of the Social World*, Evanston, IL: Northwestern University Press.

Starr, M. (2014). "Qualitative and Mixed-Methods Research in Economics: Surprising Growth, Promising Future," *Journal of Economic Surveys*, 28(2): 238–264.

Storr, V. (2004). *Enterprising Slaves and Master Pirates: Understanding Economic Life in the Bahamas*, New York: Peter Lang.

Storr, V. (2011). "On the Hermeneutics Debate: An Introduction to a Symposium on Don Lavoie's 'The Interpretive Dimension of Economics–Science, Hermeneutics, and Praxeology,'" *Review of Austrian Economics*, 24: 85–89.

Storr, V. (2013). *Understanding the Culture of Markets*, New York: Routledge.

Storr, V. H., & John, A. (2013). "Ethnicity and Self-Employment in Trinidad and Tobago: An Empirical Assessment," *International Journal of Entrepreneurship and Small Business*, 18(2): 173–193.

Swidler, A. (1986). "Culture in Action: Symbols and Strategies," *American Sociological Review*, 51(2): 273–286.

Tabellini, G. (2008). "Presidential Address: Institutions and Culture," *Journal of the European Economic Association*, 6(2–3): 255–294.

Tabellini, G. (2010). "Culture and Institutions: Economic Development in the Regions of Europe," *Journal of the European Economic Association*, 8(4): 677–716.

Throsby, D. (1999). "Cultural Capital," *Journal of Cultural Economics*, 23(1–2): 3–12.

Throsby, D. (2001). *Economics and Culture*, Cambridge; New York; Melbourne: Cambridge University Press.

Weber, M. (1951). *The Religion of China: Confucianism and Taoism*, New York: Free Press.

Weber, M. (1975) [1908]. "Marginal Utility Theory and 'The Fundamental Law of Psychophysics,'" translated by Louis Schneider, *Social Science Quarterly*, 56(1): 24–36.

Weber, M. (2002) [1905]. *The Protestant Ethic and the "Spirit" of Capitalism and Other Writings*, translated by P. Baehr and G. Wells, London: Penguin Books.

Weimann, G. (1994). "Individual Behaviour in a Free-Riding Experiment," *Journal of Public Economics*, 54(2): 185–200.

Williamson, C., & Coyne, R. (2013). "Culture and Freedom," The Annual Proceedings of the Wealth and Well-Being of Nations, Beloit College, vol. VI (2013–2014): 83–104.

Zafirovski, M. (2002). "Paths of the Weberian Austrian Interconnection," The Review of Austrian Economics, 15: 35–59.

Cambridge Elements ⁼

Austrian Economics

Peter Boettke

George Mason University

Peter Boettke is a Professor of Economics & Philosophy at George Mason University, the BB&T Professor for the Study of Capitalism, and the director of the F. A. Hayek Program for Advanced Study in Philosophy, Politics and Economics at the Mercatus Center at George Mason University.

About the Series

This series will primarily be focused on contemporary developments in the Austrian School of Economics and its relevance to the methodological and analytical debates at the frontier of social science and humanities research, and the continuing relevance of the Austrian School of Economics for the practical affairs of public policy throughout the world.

Cambridge Elements ≡

Austrian Economics

Elements in the Series

A full series listing is available at: www.cambridge.org/EAEC

CPSIA information can be obtained
at www.ICGtesting.com
Printed in the USA
LVHW080907181022
730957LV00009B/479